Messages from
Maitreya the Christ

VOLUME ONE

One Hundred Messages

THE TARA PRESS - London
TARA CENTER - Los Angeles

TARA   CENTER
P. O. Box 6001, North Hollywood, CA 91603

THE TARA PRESS
London,   England

ISBN 0-936604-01-8
Library of Congress Catalog Number 80-52483

Originally printed in booklet form in London
under the name of
Messages from Maitreya, the Christ

The painting reproduced on the cover, painted by
Benjamin Creme in 1974, represents "The Flaming
Diamond", the Greater Rod of Initiation, used at
the third and higher Initiations by Sanat Kumara,
the Lord of the World, on Shamballa. Charged at
each World Cycle from the Central Spiritual Sun,
it focusses Electrical Fire through the centres
of the Initiate. There is a "Lesser Rod" used by
the Christ at the first two Initiations.

FOREWARD

Knowingly or not, the world stands ready to recognise the Christ. His long-awaited and hoped-for reappearance is now an accomplished fact.

On July 19th, 1977, the Christ, Maitreya, the World Teacher, Head of our Spiritual Hierarchy, emerged from His ancient retreat and is now in the modern world. With His Disciples, the Masters of Wisdom, He will inaugurate the new age of synthesis and brotherhood.

"Early in September 1977 I was asked if I would take, publicly, communications from Him which, since 1974, I had received in the privacy of the group with which I work. I said I would try, do my best. On September 6th, 1977, the first public Message was given at Friends House, Euston Road, London, experimentally, to find out how I stood up to this kind of mental overshadowing and spiritual telepathy in public - a very different thing from the privacy of one's own group. These have continued until now. At the moment of going to press we have received 106 Messages.

They are conveyed by me to the audience. No trance or mediumship is involved, and the voice is mine, strengthened in power and altered in pitch by the overshadowing energy of Maitreya. They are transmitted simultaneously on all the astral and mental planes, while I supply the basic etheric-physical vibration for this to take place. From these subtle levels, the Messages impress the minds and hearts of countless people who are gradually made aware of the thoughts and the Presence of the Christ. A great thoughtform is being built, on the inner planes, embodying the fact of the Christ's Presence. This thought-form is then tuned into by the sensitives, clairvoyants and mediums of the world who from now on will increasingly bring in (in more or less distorted form) the information of the Christ's return. He releases in this way frag- ments of His Teaching, to prepare the climate of hope and expectancy which will ensure His being accepted and followed, quickly and gladly.

It is an enormous and embarrassing claim to have to make - that the Christ is giving messages through oneself. But if people can rid their minds of the idea of the Christ as some sort of spirit, sitting in "heaven" at God's right hand; if they can begin to see Him as indeed He is, as a real and living man (albeit a Divine man) who has never left the world; who descended not from "heaven" but from His ancient retreat in the Himalayas, to complete the task He began in Palestine; as a great Master, an Adept and Yogi; as the chief actor in a Gospel Story which is essentially true, but much simpler than hitherto presented. If people can accept that possibility, then the claim to receive telepathic communica- tions from such a closer and more knowable Being is also, perhaps, more acceptable. In any case, I leave it to a study of the quality of the Messages themselves to convince or otherwise. For many people, the energies which flow during the overshadowing convince. Many who come to the meetings at which these Messages are given are clairvoyant in various degrees, and their visions of the overshadowing as it takes place is for them the most convincing evidence of all."

The previous statement is extracted from the preface to "The Reappearance of the Christ and the Masters of Wisdom" by Benjamin Creme. Tara Press 1980.

Through these communications Maitreya, the Christ, suggests the lines that social change must take. He gives hints on how to recognise Him and urges His listeners to make known the fact of His Presence. He evokes also the desire to share and to serve humanity and Him.

It is interesting to note how He returns to His themes again and again, presenting them differently and with growing emphasis. It is interesting, too, to see how every tenth Message - Nos. 10, 20, 30, and so on - stands out from the others; how in these He describes Himself in abstract terms as the Embodiment of Divine Qualities rather than as the simple man, the brother and friend of humanity, which He is at pains to emphasise elsewhere.

It is recommended that readers take one Message at a time and read it aloud. In this way the rhythmic (mantric) quality of each Message can be better felt. It is almost impossible to say these Messages aloud, with attention, without invoking the Christ's energy, His heart response. They are apparently simple, sent from heart to heart, but work on various levels and should be meditated upon for their full meaning to come through. Some people find it best to select one Message daily and meditate on that.

Many, singly and in groups, use in their meditations the tapes from which these Messages are transcribed. The Christ's energies, magnetised on to the tape as the Message is given, are released again at each re-playing, thus enhancing the quality of the meditation.

BENJAMIN CREME

London - June 1980

ADDITIONAL BOOKS BY BENJAMIN CREME

The Reappearance of the Christ and the Masters of Wisdom - 256 p. quality paperback, $5.00

Covers background and pertinent information regarding the reappearance and emergence of the Christ into full public view. A vast range of questions is covered: from the esoteric view of the Christ and the Turin Shroud to the problems of the Third World and a new economic order; from UFOs and Atlantis to healing and meditation.

Maitreya the Christ - 40 p. booklet, $1.50

A condensed version of the above book including a number of sample messages from this book, recently up-dated to include an appendix on how the emergence is proceeding. It gives an overview as well as eight messages from the Christ. This is an informative and inexpensive way to share the message with friends and relatives.

Cassette and video tapes of public lectures are also available plus cassette tapes of the messages as they were originally received by Benjamin Creme.

For additional information, please write to

TARA CENTER
P. O. Box 6001
North Hollywood, CA 91603
U.S.A.

Message No. 1

September 6th 1977

My dear friends, it will not be long until you
see My face.
When that time comes I shall take your hands in
Mine and lead you to Him Whom we serve together.

My Manifestation is complete and accomplished.
I am, verily, in the world.

Soon you shall know Me, perhaps follow Me and
love Me.
My Love flows ever through you all.
And that Love, which I hold for all mankind,
has brought Me here.

My brothers and sisters, My return to the world
is a signal that the New Age, as you call it,
has commenced.

In this coming time, I shall show you Beauties
and Wonders beyond your imaginings, but which
are your birthright, as Sons of God.

My children, My friends, I have come more
quickly, perhaps, than you expected.
But there is much to do, much that needs
changing in the world.
Many hunger and die,
many suffer needlessly.

I come to change all that;
to show you the way forward - into a simpler,
saner, happier life - together.
No longer man against man,
nation against nation,
but together, as brothers, shall we go forth
into the New Country.

And those who are ready shall see the Father's Face.

May the Divine Love and Light and Power of the One God be now manifest within your hearts and minds.
May this Light and Love and Power lead you to seek That which dwells always in your heart's centre.
Find That, and make It manifest.

Message No. 2

September 15th 1977

Good evening, My dear friends.

I have taken, again, this opportunity to speak
to you, and to establish firmly in your minds
the reasons for My return.

There are many reasons why I should descend
and appear once more among you.
Chiefly they are as follows:

My Brothers, the Masters of Wisdom, are
scheduled to make Their group return to the
everyday world.
As Their Leader, I, as one of Them, do likewise.

Many there are throughout the world who call Me,
beg for My return.
I answer their pleas.

Many more are hungry and perish needlessly, for
want of the food which lies rotting in the
storehouses of the world.

Many need My help in other ways:
as Teacher, Protector; as Friend and Guide.

It is as all of these I come.

To lead men, if they will accept Me, into the
New Time, the New Country, the glorious future
which awaits humanity in this coming Age;

For all of this I come.

12

I come, too, to show you the Way to God, back
to your Source;
to show you that the Way to God is a simple
path which all men can tread;

To lead you upwards, into the Light of that new
TRUTH which is the REVELATION that I bring.

For all of this I come.

Let me take you by the hand and lead you into
that beckoning Country, to show you the marvels,
the glories of God, which are yours to behold.

The vanguard of My Masters of Wisdom are now
among you.
Soon you will know Them.
Help Them in Their work.
Know, too, that They are building the New Age,
through you.
Let Them lead and guide, show you the way;
and in doing this you will have served
your brothers and sisters well.

Take heart, My friends.
All will be well.
All manner of things will be well.

Good night, My dear friends.

May the Divine Light and Love and Power of the
One God be now manifest within your hearts and
minds.
May this manifestation lead you to seek That
which dwells ever within you.
Find That, and know God.

Message No. 3

September 22nd 1977

Good evening, My dear friends.

I am happy to be able to speak to you once more,
and to tell you that I come to take you with Me
into the New Country - the Country of Love,
the Country of Trust, of Beauty and Freedom.

I shall take you there if you can follow Me,
accept Me, let Me lead and guide.
And, if this be so, together we shall build
a New World:

A world in which men can live without fear,
without mistrust, without division;
sharing together the Earth's bounty,
knowing together the Bliss of Union with our
Source.

All this can be yours.
You have only to take the first steps and I
may lead.

Allow Me to help you.
Allow Me to show you the way - forward, into
a simpler life where no man lacks;
where no two days are alike;
where the Joy of Brotherhood manifests through
all men.

Mine is the task to lead and guide, but you,
willingly, must follow.
Otherwise, I can do nothing. My hands are tied
by Law.

The decision rests with mankind.

May the Divine Light and Love and Power of the
One God be now manifest within your hearts and
minds.
May this manifestation lead you to seek and to
find That which dwells ever within you.
Identify with That and know God.

Message No. 4

September 29th 1977

My dear friends, I am pleased indeed to be able
to speak to you once more in this fashion.

Many await My Coming with reverence and also
with some fear.
This is inevitable.

My coming will mean the end of the old order of
things.
All that is useless, no longer serving the
purposes of Man, can now be discarded.

This will cause many to grieve
but so it must be.

My friends, My children, I am here to show you
that there exists for Man a most marvellous
future.
Decked in all the colours of the rainbow, glowing
with the Light of God, Man, one day, will stand
upright in His Divinity.
This I promise you.

I am a simple Man, and simply I make My appeal
to you:
Trust Me, follow Me, let Me take you into the
future time,
on the basis of LOVE,
on the basis of SHARING,
on the basis of BROTHERHOOD.

Let Me show you the way into that state of simple
interdependence, of justice, correct alignment
with your Source and your brothers.

Many will heed Me, but not all.
Nevertheless, My Army of Light will surely
triumph.

Many will see Me soon and know Me not.
Many will see Me soon and recognise Me.
They are My People.
Be you one of them.

My heart flows with Love for you all.

May the Divine Light and Love and Power of the
One God be now manifest within your hearts and
minds.
May this manifestation lead you to seek and to
know that Self which is God.

Message No. 5

October 4th 1977

Good evening, My dear friends.
I am pleased indeed to have this further
opportunity to speak to you in this way.

My aim is to make known My Presence in the
world at the earliest possible moment, and so
begin My Work in the full light of day.
This will mean strenuous work by those who
now accept that I am among you.
Make known to all that I am here,
and pave smooth My Path.

My Plan is to release into the world a certain
Teaching, which will show men that there exists
a new approach to Living, a new way forward
into the future time.

May you be among the first to recognise Me,
and through you I may work.

Take upon yourselves this task.
There is none higher which you could do in this
life.
Commit yourself to this work and serve your
brothers.
I am desirous that the world should know of My
Presence, should quickly accept Me, and,
hopefully, follow My lead.

I am sure that you will not fail Me.
I am certain that you will not reject this
privilege, this gift of service;
but will willingly take it upon your shoulders,
to ease the burden of My Task.

My Blessings are upon you all.

May the Divine Light and Love and Power of the
One God be now manifest within your hearts and
minds.
May this manifestation lead you to know that
God dwells ever within you.
Find That and make It manifest.

Message No. 6

October 10th 1977

Good evening, My dear friends.
Once again, I have the pleasure of speaking to
you in this way.

Very little time indeed now separates Me from
you, in full vision.
Mankind will see Me very soon.

And, if they follow Me, I shall lead them forward
into the future which awaits them;
a future bathed in the Light of Truth, of Harmony,
and Love.

My friends, I would ask you to help Me,
to take upon yourselves a share of the burden of
preparation.
If you can accept that I am here, make known this
fact wherever you find a listener.

It may be that you will see Me without knowing Me.
It may be that you will walk the other way.

But, if this be so, you will forfeit a Treasure
unlike that which you might build in a thousand
lifetimes.

Make it your task to tell men that I am here,
that I am working for them, for their future,
for the future of all men and all things in the
world.

Make known My Presence among you,
and be delivered of all that is useless in the
past.

Make known My Presence,
and be assured that My Love will flow through
you and light a path before you for your
brothers and sisters.
Do this work and help them and Me.

My Task is but beginning.
When completed, I shall look back on this
time as one of kindling Light in the hearts
of the few who sought to serve their brothers.
May you be one of them.

My heartfelt Love flows to you all.

May the Divine Light and Love and Power of the
One God be now manifest within your hearts and
minds.
May this manifestation lead you to seek That
which lies hidden but ever ready to shine
forth.
Find That and know God.

Message No. 7

October 20th 1977

Good evening, My dear friends, I am happy indeed
to speak to you once more in this way.

My Plan is working out, but will entail the
greatest service and sacrifice from those among
you who accept that I am in the world.

If you can make known this fact on a wide
enough scale, it will not be long indeed till
the world knows My Face.

My aim is to shorten this time yet further, but
an early declaration of My Presence depends on
you, depends on your will to serve.

Become My People, and do this work for Me.
Become My Friends, and serve your brothers.
Become My Children, and know God.

This is no easy task I set you for men are blind.
But when mankind knows that I am here I am
certain that it will respond from its heart,
and let Me lead.

My People are everywhere.
Join them.
Become one of them.
Make this life a crowning achievement, and take
part in the Great Plan.

I ask you to do this because you have come into
the world for this.

You are here, not by chance, but to serve at
this time your brothers and sisters.
Seize then this opportunity, presented to
you with love.

My Blessings are upon you all.

May the Divine Light and Love and Power of the
One God be now manifest within your hearts and
minds.
May this manifestation lead you to know that
God dwells ever within you.
Seek within, and make It manifest.

Message No. 8

October 27th 1977

Once more I have the pleasure of speaking to you
in this way.

My intention is to reveal Myself 'ere long, to
send My Teaching into the world through My
People,
those who know Me,
who love Me,
and through whom I work.

This is the first phase of My Plan.
Then will follow Myself in full vision, known
and recognised or not.
When the world is ready to receive Me, I shall
speak to men everywhere
as the One Who is awaited,
the One they have called,
the One Who comes to lead them into the New Age.

My Mission is but beginning,
yet, already, there are the signs of response, of
recognition that My Advent is nigh.
Many there are, now, throughout the world who feel
My Presence,
who stand open and ready for My Teaching.

When I make Myself known, I shall express the hope
of all mankind for a new life, a new start, a
readiness to change direction;
to see the construction of a New World in which
men can live in peace;
can live free from fear of themselves or their
brothers;
free to create from the joy in their hearts;
free to be themselves, in simple honesty.

My Task is but beginning,
but even now there exists in men's hearts a
new light, a new hope, a sense of a new beginning;
a realisation that Man is not alone,
that the Protector of All has sent His Agent.
It is That which I am.

May the Blessings of Him be upon you all.

May the Divine Light and Love and Power of the
One God, Protector of All, be now manifest within
your hearts and minds.
May this manifestation lead you to know that you
are never without the close Presence and Guidance
of God.

Message No. 9

Good evening, My dear friends. I am happy
to be with you once more in this fashion,
and to tell you that My return in full vision
will not be long delayed.

Full well do I know the problems which beset
mankind.
Full well do I see the changes required.
But also I see in Man the desire to know,
to lift his consciousness, and to see through
the clouds.

It is this urge to know which is Man's great
gift.
When men know the Way to God, this gift will
flower in creative magnificence.

My purpose tonight is to tell you that My
Masters are with you already, are guiding and
magnetising the work of Their groups.
It may be that you yourselves will soon find
this stimulus, recognise it for what it is,
and seek to help the Plan.

My Army of Light is assembled, is ready.
Banners flying, eyes uplifted, they march
forward into the future,
into the Light which beckons,
and in that Light shall they see Light.

Many there are who doubt My Presence.
This is natural; men are blind.
But soon there will be no gainsaying.
My efforts will show men
that the wheel turns,
that soon the New Time, the New World, will have
commenced.

May it be that you will share in this work.

My Blessings are upon you all.

May the Divine Light and Love and Power of the
One and Holy God be now manifest within your
hearts and minds.
May this manifestation lead you to seek and to
find That which dwells ever within you.
Know That as the Self, and make It manifest.

Message No. 10

November 8th 1977

I am among you once more, My dear friends.

I come to tell you that you will see Me very
soon, each in his own way.
Those who look for Me in terms of My Beloved
Disciple, the Master Jesus, will find His
qualities in Me.
Those who look for Me as a Teacher are nearer
the mark, for that is what I am.
Those who search for signs will find them, but
My method of manifestation is more simple.

Nothing separates you from Me, and soon many
will realise this.
I am with you and in you.
I seek to express that which I am through you;
for this I come.

Many will follow Me and see Me as their Guide.
Many will know Me not.
My aim is to enter into the life of all men
and through them change that life.
Be ready to see Me soon;
be ready to hear My words,
to follow My thoughts,
to heed My plea.

I am the Stranger at the Gate.
I am the One Who knocks.
I am the One Who will not go away.

I am your Friend.
I am your Hope.
I am your Shield.
I am your Love.
I am All in All.

Take Me into yourselves, and let Me work through
you.
Make Me part of yourselves, and show Me to the
world.
Allow Me to manifest through you, and know God.

May the Divine Light and Love and Power of the
One and Holy God be now manifest within your
hearts and minds.
May this manifestation lead you to know that
God dwells silently, now and forever, within
you all.

Message No. 11

January 5th 1978

My dear friends, I am happy to be with you once more.

My Plan is that My Teaching should precede My Presence and prepare My Way. My people will release it through their groups and group endeavour.
When mankind is somewhat prepared My Voice shall be heard.

Meanwhile, My efforts are bearing fruit, producing change, drawing together men and nations, and bringing new hope to the world.

I am emerging soon, but first I would point the way into the new direction which Man, if he would survive, must take.

Firstly, men must see themselves as brothers, sons of the One Father.
This is essential if they would progress one step nearer The Godhead.
Throughout the world there are men, women and little children who have not even the essentials to stay alive; they crowd the cities of many of the poorest countries in the world.
This crime fills Me with shame.
My brothers, how can you watch these people die before your eyes and call yourselves men?
My Plan is to save these, My little ones, from certain starvation and needless death.

My Plan is to show you that the way out of your
problems is to listen again to the true voice of
God within your hearts, to share the produce of
this most bountiful of worlds among your brothers
and sisters everywhere.

I need your help, I call on you to aid Me in My
task.
How can I stand aside and watch this slaughter,
watch My little ones die?
No, My friends, this cannot be.
Therefore I am come quickly among you once more
to show you the way, point the path.
But the success of My Mission depends on you:
you must make the choice - whether you share
and learn to live peacefully as True Men, or
perish utterly.
My heart tells Me your answer, your choice, and
is glad.

May the Divine Light and Love and Power of the
One Most Holy God fall now upon your hearts and
minds.
May this Light, Love and Power lead you to seek
That which dwells in silence within you.
Find That and know that you are Gods.

Message No. 12

January 10th 1978

My dear friends, I am happy to be with you once
more, and to reveal to you My thoughts on Man's
problem.

Man's problem today, as always, is of his own
making; it is not inherent in the Plan of God.
By the misuse of his divine freewill Man has
placed his future, and that of all the kingdoms,
in jeopardy.
Many today are beginning to realise this and
are taking such steps as they can to avert
catastrophe.
This is good.
But not all men see the danger which faces
mankind in increasing potency. Time is short
indeed for the reconstruction of our world
along lines more befitting Man's true role and
purpose.
My task is to show you the way, outline the
possibilities only, for by Man himself must
the New World be forged.

There are many today who admit the necessity
for change, but still resist it.
There are many today who see the crumbling of
the old and outworn world of the past, but
cling to the old forms.

But there is a new voice being heard among the
nations: the voice of Truth, which contains the
hope, the promise, of the New Time.
This voice will increasingly make its impress
on the minds of men, for it is the voice of God,
speaking through men.

32

My Masters are with you and will show you the way,
I Myself will lead.
Can it be that you will renounce this guidance,
this opportunity to rise and progress?
No, My friends, I think not.
I shall show you that the way for Man is the way
of brotherhood, close co-operation and mutual
trust and service.
This is the only way. All else has failed.
My friends, unless Man can do this, Man on this
Earth will cease to be.
I threaten not but simply state the truth.
There is but little time left to restore the
balance of nature and the world.

Make it your primary task to release to all men
the wherewithal to exist in human dignity, as
Sons of God, Brothers all.
Make over, in trust for all men, the produce of
the world to the nations of the world.
Do this today as free men and reap the glory
tomorrow as True Sons of God.

May the Divine Light and Love and Power of the
One Most Holy God fall now upon your hearts and
minds.
May this Light, Love and Power show you to
yourselves as very God.

Message No. 13

January 19th 1978

My dear friends, I am happy indeed to be with you
once more in this way.

My mission is proceeding according to plan and,
if all goes well, you will soon hear My Voice.
Meanwhile I would say this:
Mankind has lost its way, has strayed far from
the path prepared for it by God.
Many there are now in the world who know this,
who search and pray, and work towards the Light;
but many more are blind and would rush towards
disaster.
My Plan is to halt this headlong plunge and to
turn the tide.

My Presence, already, is effecting changes in
men's thinking, in men's hearts, and causing
them to wonder.
My efforts are proving effective despite all
appearances. Men are turning again to the Truth,
to the Laws which are God.

Allow Me to show you the way into the New Time;
to outline for you the glories, which if you will,
can be yours.
Man is made to serve both God and Man, and only
through that correct service can the path to God
be trodden.
Make it your task to take upon yourselves the
task of re-orientation, reconstruction and change.

Each man is a lighthouse and sheds abroad his
light for his brother. Make bright your lamp
and let it shine forth and show the way.
All are needed, every one. No one is too small
or young to take part in this great Plan for
the rescue and the rehabilitation of our world.
Resolve to do this and be assured that My help
will not be withheld.

How to start?
Begin by dedicating yourself and all that you
are and have been to the service of the world,
to the service of your brothers and sisters
everywhere.
Make sure that not one day passes without some
act of true service and be assured that My help
will be yours.
This, the Path of Service, is the only path for
True Men, for it is the path which leads them
to God.

My People are drawing together around Me,
responding to My Call, and are achieving more
than they could know.
Together we shall fashion a new and better world.
May you be open and ready for My Call when it
comes.

My Blessings are upon you all.

May the Divine Light and Love and Power of the
One Most Holy God be now within your hearts and
minds.
May this Divine Light and Love and Power lead
you to become That which you are,
True Sons of God.

Message No. 14

I am with you once more, My dear friends.

My Army of Light is on the march and soon the
Great Battle will have begun.
My People are preparing My Way and will show
you My Plan.
My Masters of Wisdom are now assembling Their
various groups and soon the world will know
that I am here.
My Army has laid its plans and soon will
follow results. Already the signs of change
are appearing, the clouds are lifting, and a
new hope seizes mankind.

Will you be among those who pave the way?
Will you take part now in this great work and
fulfil the world's need?
There is no higher call than that to serve
the world.
There is no greater commitment than to serve
your brother.
Hold fast to the purpose of your return and
help My Plan.
Many there are who hear Me and heed Me not,
but the few have listened and with Will and
Love fulfil My Task.

There is now assembling a vast army of
individuals who together form My Vanguard.
They know Me whether they know Me or not.

They follow Me whether they realise that I am
here or am still to come.
They need Me as I need them.
They are Me as I am in them.
Make yourselves one of those through whom I may
work and reveal Myself.
Take up that challenge and fulfil this life.
Can you not hear the drums calling you into the
future?
Can you be deaf to their thunder?
Make now the choice to serve and grow, or forever
to regret.

May the Divine Light and Love and Power of the
One Most Holy God be now manifest within your
hearts and minds.
May this manifestation lead you to seek and to
discover the Glory of God which within you dwells.

My dear friends, I am with you once more.

I am happy to be able to tell you that My plans proceed smoothly and well.
My Vanguard is preparing mankind and very little time now remains till My Face is seen.
I would have you know that I expect all My People, My devoted ones, to work for Me, to prepare somewhat My Way.

Many there are now who would gladly know that I am here. Tell them.
Tell them that the Son of Man has returned, that their Elder Brother is among them, that the long wait is over, and fresh and eager for the battle has come their Friend and Leader.
Tell them this, and offer them, too, the opportunity to serve the Plan.

Many will see Me soon and at first may be surprised at My Appearance, for I am not the preacher of old; but have come simply to point the way, to show the path which must be trodden, back to the Source and into Harmony, Beauty, and Justice.

My task is a simple one: to show you the way.
You, My friends, have the difficult task of building a new world, a new country, a new truth; but together we shall triumph.

There are Those among you now who know the Way,
have walked the Path before, and can lead and
save.
My Brothers, the Masters of Wisdom are your
friends and guides.
They will be among you and serve you and
inspire you to great deeds, valiant acts; and
They bring precious gifts of Wisdom and Love
to place at your feet.

There is only one way to God and that, My
friends, you already know.
The way to God is the way of Brotherhood, of
Justice and Love.
There is no other way; all is contained therein.
Many will find this path bitter and hard;
but many more, by far, will enter upon this
path with joy and gladness at the lightness
of their burden, casting away the old, the
outworn and the useless, the trivia of the past;
and entering into shared brotherhood and joyous
communion with all that is, that vast and
growing company shall inherit their Selfhood.

May the Divine Light and Love and Power of the
One and Holy God be now manifest within your
hearts and minds.
May this manifestation lead you to know that
within you dwells, now and forever, that God
which is your Self.

Message No. 16

February 7th 1978

My dear friends, I am happy to be with you once
more.

My Plan is to reveal to men that there exists
for them but two paths.
One will lead them inexorably to devastation
and death.
The other, My friends, My dear ones, will lead
mankind straight to God; and in the light of
His Presence they, if ready, will see wonders
and unbelievable glories.

My Task is to point the way, to lead you out of
discord into that blessed state of Harmony and
Love which will vouchsafe to you that dream.
My Work proceeds, and soon, now very soon, you
will see My Face and hear My Words.

The period of test begins.
My Plan is to place before you these two
alternatives, to outline the possibilities and
the pitfalls.
The choice is yours; you, from your own divinely
given freewill, must decide.
If you, as in My Heart I know you will, decide
for God, I shall take you to Him; and together
we shall place before Him our life of service
to Him and to the world.
Many of My People, already, are so doing.
It is this which confers on them the appellation,
"My Beloved Ones".
Join this band of true servers of the world.

Become My Workers;
become My Companions;
become My Heroes, and serve the Plan.

Little time remains for this work of
preparation. Take now the first steps into
your glory.
Serve the purpose of your return and the Plan
of God; they are one and the same.
My Masters will show you the first steps out
of the quagmire. They will show you that a
simpler life can be led in full happiness
and manifested Divinity, through love and
service of our brothers.
This is the Way of Old; it is the Way of all
time; nothing really changes with God.
Make now your choice: to serve My Plan and see
the Light which beckons you into the future, or
to sound forever the knell of regret.

May the Divine Light and Love and Power of the
One Most Holy God be now manifest within your
hearts and minds.
May this manifestation lead you to look within
and there to find that God Who forever in you
dwells.

Good evening, My dear friends, I am happy to be
with you once more, in this way.

Soon My Appearance will be known to many and My
Teaching will have begun.
Mankind will be faced by Me with two lines of
action; on their decision rests the future of
this world.
I will show them that the only possible choice
is through sharing and mutual interdependence.
By this means, Man will come into that state of
awareness of himself and his purpose which will
lead him to the feet of God.
The other way is too terrible to contemplate,
for it would mean the annihilation of all life-
streams on this Earth.

Man has the future in his hands.
Weigh well, oh Men, and if you choose as True
Men would, I may lead you into the Light of your
Divine inheritance.
Make your choice well and let Me lead.
Make your choice well and be assured of My
continuing succour.
Make your choice well, My brothers, and be
delivered of all that holds you in limitation.

My Army is on the move, is marching bravely
into the future. Join those who already fight
on the side of Light, on the side of Truth, of
Freedom and Justice.
Join My Vanguard and show the way for your
brothers.

Many there are who sense that I am here, yet
speak not. Why hold this knowledge to yourself
when your brothers cry for light, for wisdom,
and help?
Allow them, too, to share in the joy of the
Promise which I bring. Tell them, My friends,
that you believe that Maitreya has come; that
the Lord of Love is here;
that the Son of Man walks again among His
brothers.
Tell them that soon My Face will be seen, My
Words will be heard; and in the seeing and the
hearing they are tested and known.

May the Divine Light and Love and Power of the
One Most Holy God be now manifest within your
hearts and minds.
May this manifestation lead you to seek and
to find that Divine Source from which you came.

Message No. 18

February 23rd 1978

My dear friends, I am indeed happy to be with
you once more.

My Face will soon be seen, My Words heard.
When you see Me you will know that you have not
waited in vain.
You will know that your Brother of Old has come
to share your life.

Liberation is the goal for mankind.
To that goal I shall point the way, shall lead
you forward and cut before you the steps of
ascent.
My Masters will show you how to live simply and
well and in full happiness.
They have trodden the road before and know well
the Way.
Like children in full trust let Them show you
that Way; let Them take you step by step through
the labyrinth.
And when you are ready, before My Splendor shall
you come and through Me shall you see the Face
of God.

Make your choice well, My friends; make it now.
Take your stand with those who wish to share
and love, with those for whom Justice is divine.
Make now your choice and let your light shine
forth and ease My Path.

Men await My Coming yet know not that I am
already here.
Tell them that My Manifestation is completed.
I, Maitreya, their Brother, stand among them.

Await my Call, and act.
Tell men that I expect that they will follow Me,
but they must decide.
They must want the path which they must tread
if they would see God.

May the Divine Light and Love and Power of the
One Most Holy God be now manifest within your
hearts and minds.
May this manifestation lead you to seek and to
find that Joy and Peace which forever in you
dwells.

Message No. 19

February 28th 1978

Good evening, My dear friends, I am happy
indeed to be with you once more and to tell you
that I emerge forthwith.

The time of My Coming is over.
The time of My Emergence has arrived; and soon,
now, in full vision and fact, My Face and Words
will become known.
May you quickly recognise Me, My dear friends,
My dear ones, and help your brothers to do
likewise.

I am your Friend and Brother, not a God.
It is true My Father has, once again, sent Me
to you; but I come to you who are My Brethren;
to guide you and lead you, if you will, into a
blessed future.
My Task will be to show that for mankind the
ways part.
The Signposts are set, and on your decision
rests the future of this Earth.
We are here together, you and I, to ensure that
Man chooses the correct path, the only Way which
can lead him to God.

You are here because in your heart you are
responding to My Call, to the fact of My
Presence, knowingly or not.
Make it then your task to tell the others,
to point to the simple way of Truth which
beckons mankind.
Teach men that to share is divine;
to love is God's nature;

to work together is Man's destiny.
Take your stand on the only platform from which
the Light of the future may be seen.
Take your stand My friends, together, and show
the Way.

Many of you will see Me soon.
Share with your brothers this joyous expectation
and tell them that Maitreya, their Friend, their
Brother, their Teacher of Old, has come.
Do this now and restore to men the hope which
they have lost.
Do this now and work for Me.
Work in service to the world and stand in the
Blessing of My Love.

May the Divine Light and Love and Power of the
One Most Holy God be now manifest within your
hearts and minds.
May this manifestation reveal to you that you
are, now and forever, sons of the only living
God.

Message No. 20

March 7th 1978

My dear friends, I am happy indeed to be with
you once more in this fashion.

My Plan is that My Face and Words shall be known
forthwith.
My Emergence begins.
May it be that you will quickly sense My
Presence, seek Me out and share My burden,
for My Plan involves you all.
There is little that I can do without your help,
your eager participation and acceptance of
service.
Through you, if you know Me, love Me, love My
Work, answer My Call, that Work may be done.
I need helpers.
I seek to place before you the chance to grow in
service, to lift yourselves upward into a new
light, into a new responsibility, and when I
call I shall expect you.
Many there are now who are doing this work for
Me yet know Me not, nor know that I am here.
It has always been so, for many work better in
the shade.
But you, My friends, have the opportunity for
full and conscious service.
Seize it then and begin now.
Take part in a Great Plan which is changing the
world, which is drawing together all men and
all nations, which is showing the way into the
future and back to God.

Many of you have heard this Call before, yet
still resist action.

Nothing will happen by chance.
It is a call to action that I give and that
action will I potentise, manyfold.
Take now this chance to be My Disciples, to
be My Friends, My True Men.

Before My Coming men knew no way out; stuck
fast in the quagmire of their problems, they
feared.
Today there is a new light, a new possibility
for change.
A new hope is sweeping the world: that is My
Ray, My Gift to you, My Blessing to all men.

May the Divine Light and Love and Power of the
One Most Holy God be now manifest within you
all.

Message No. 21

March 14th 1978

My dear friends, I am with you once more.

I wish to tell you that My Presence in the world
will soon be known to many, My Face seen and My
Teaching heard.

I am with you in many ways:
I am with you as Maitreya, the Leader of My
Group of Masters.
I am with you as the Embodiment of that Divine
Force which you call the Christ Principle.
I am with you as your Brother of Old, as the
Eldest of our Family.
I am with you as God's Representative, as the
Spokesman for that Divine Being Whose dreams we
are.
I shall take you to Him when you are ready, when
you have passed through the Gates twice, and
stood shining before Me.

My friends, I am with you and in you and around
you.
I am the Lord of Love.
I am the Hope of Mankind.
I am the Well.
I am your Bliss.
I am returned to you by the One we call God

May the Divine Light and Love and Power of the
One Most Holy God be now manifest within your
hearts and minds.
May this manifestation lead you to seek and to
know that Divine Self which, now and forever,
you are.

Message No. 22

March 22nd 1978

I am with you once more, My dear friends.

I am here to tell you that My Emergence has
commenced, and before long you will see Me and
hear My words.

There are those among you who know that I am
here, who see Me in their visions and dreams,
yet speak not.
Why hold this wonder to yourselves?
My people cry for truth, for light and succour.
Let them know that I am returned, that I am
here, working and planning for them; to take them,
if they will, back to the Father, onward into the
future, upward into the Light.
Tell them that I am among them and soon will they
see Me. Tell them this.

My Plans work smoothly, and soon you will see a
great transformation in the world.
Despite the signs, the changes are occuring.
Despite the tension, My Love is spread abroad.
Know this and be at peace within yourselves and
raise the hope of men.

I am here with you now, My dear friends, and ask
you to give Me your allegiance, your trust, your
help.

To show men that the way into the future lies
through Love and Justice, have I come.
To take men into that future and to show them
the Ways of God, am I here.
Be, then, My dear ones, ready to receive Me,
to work with Me, to dispel the fog of fear and
ignorance which enshrouds mankind.
Take, then, My hand, and let Me lead you into
that golden future in which those who are ready
shall see the Face of God.
My Blessing goes with you all.

May the Divine Light and Love and Power of the
One Most Holy God be now manifest within your
hearts and minds.
May this manifestation lead you to seek and to
find that Divine Being Whom in truth you are.

Message No. 23

March 28th 1978

Good evening, My dear friends, I am happy to
be with you once more and to reveal to you My
Plan for the immediate future time.

My Plan is to make known My Face in full and
visible fact, to reach you through My Words,
to receive from you your allegiance and
help.
Nought can be done by Me without this
willing help, for you, My friends, must
remake the world.
I shall send My Disciples to you, and They
will show you the way; but you must act and
follow Our Plan.

My Teaching will proceed from now. Gradually
men will know of My Presence, take heed, and
begin to follow a new course.
My hope is that you will quickly gather
yourselves around Me, wherever you may be,
and take your stand by My side.
Men and women throughout the world, who
share My hope for a new life for men, will
lead the way; and together we shall make
safe the world.

My Vanguard has been preparing mankind for
this time.
There are few in the world who know not in
their hearts that My Return is nigh. On all
levels this truth resounds.

You will find this to be so when you make
your approach to your brothers.
Each one of you in his heart has seen the
new light which beckons from afar, which
holds the Promise of the future time.
That light will grow into a flame unseen
before on Earth, when mankind takes the
Path which will lead him back to God.
That Path it is My Mission to unfold
before your advancing feet and point the
Way to God.

May the Divine Light and Love and Power
of the One Most Holy God be now manifest
within your hearts and minds.
May this manifestation lead you out of the
labyrinth into the Light; that you might
grow in that Light, and see a higher Light.

Message No. 24

April 4th 1978

My dear friends, I am happy to be with you
once more in this way.

Soon will you see Me in full fact.
My Presence will become known to you, and, if
your response is as I hope, we shall meet and
work together as friends.
My intention is to place before you the answers
to Man's dilemma, to show you that the future
holds for all men unbelievable promise.
With My Brothers, the Masters of Wisdom, I
shall show you the way to release your divinity
and receive your inheritance.

My Plan is to awaken Mankind to its true worth,
its true capacity, and show it that within
all men lives a divine Son of God.
If men will follow Me, I shall take them
step by step through the process of Initiation,
whose Seal I guard.
In this way they will reveal the God Who
within them dwells.

My Masters are preparing the way.
They are choosing Their workers through whom
to act, and soon, in the Centres, the fiat will
go forth, the work will commence, and the New
Dispensation for Mankind will begin.

You who are here present are among those who
can point the way. Show to your brothers
that there exists for Man a better life, a
better future than he could dream of.
Tell them that Maitreya lives,
that the Lord of Love walks abroad,
that the Son of Man is returned to the
world, to change that world, through men.
Tell them this My friends, and reveal to
them the hope of the future.

May the Divine Light and Love and Power of
the One Most Holy God be now manifest
within your hearts and minds. May this
manifestation lead you to seek and to find
that God Whom forever you have been.

Message No. 25

April 11th 1978

My dear friends, I am with you once more.
I can tell you now that there are those
among your brothers and sisters who have
seen My Face. My Name as yet is unknown
to them but My Presence is a living reality
to them.
May this soon be so for you.

My Masters are gathering together Their
forces, Their Groups, and in focussed
strength We move forward into the future,
into the light of a new day.
My aim is to take you with Me into that
clear light, and to spread before your eyes
the wonders of God.
Take heart from these words, My friends,
and follow Me.
Let Me lift you upwards into your true
stature as Sons of God, as True Men, brothers
all.
I hold out My hands towards you, ready to
receive you with love, to show you the way
which all men must sometime tread.
Take then, My hands, My dear ones, and let
me lead.

Make known to all that I am here, that I am
returned and prepare men for the Day of
Declaration, the Day of God's Gift; for on
that day men will celebrate together the
achievement of God's Will.
My Coming is nothing less.

Take now your stand at My side, and let us
together prove that Man is God,
that there is nothing which is other than
God.

May the Divine Light and Love and Power of
the One Most Holy God be now manifest
within your hearts and minds.
May this manifestation lead you to realise
your true nature as Sons of God.

Message No. 26

April 18th 1978

My dear friends, I am happy to be with you once more.

I am indeed among you, in a new way: your brothers and sisters know Me, have seen Me and call Me friend and brother.

My Plan is to reveal Myself stage by stage, and to draw together around Me those enlightened souls through whom I may work. This process has begun, and soon, in My Centre, My Presence will become known.

My body of workers will show the world that the problems of Mankind can be solved; through the process of sharing and just redistribution the needs of all can be met. This growing group will show men that there is but little need for the suffering of so many, for the hunger, disease and anguish which beset mankind.

My Plan is to take you on a journey into a New Country, a new approach to living in which all men can share.
Let Me lead you, let Me show you the way, let Me lift you upwards into the Light of a new Truth.
Let Me show you, My friends, the Way to God, for only through the manifestation of God's Will can God be known.
I am here to administer that Will.

Take this opportunity to serve and grow
in service, My friends, for none greater
has been offered to any man.
Take this opportunity to serve, and see
the Face of Him we call God.

My arms are held towards you My friends,
asking for your trust, appealing for your
help in remaking your world.
Many are the tasks which lie ahead, many
are the blows which must be struck for
Freedom and Truth.
I need all those in whom that Truth shines
to follow Me and help Me in My work.
May you be ready when you hear My Call.
That Call will resound in the ears of men
everywhere, throughout the world. It is
a Call to God.

May the Divine Light and Love and Power of
the One Most Holy God be now manifest within
your hearts and minds.
May this manifestation lead you to seek and
to know that Essence of God which in Truth
you are.

Message No. 27

April 25th 1978

I am happy to be with you again, My dear
friends, and to tell you that My Emergence
proceeds to plan.

There are many now among your brothers who
know Me well, who trust Me, whose Advocate
I shall become.

Make haste to welcome Me, to know Me, to
share My Burden.
Those among you who wish to serve the world
have placed before them now the opportunity
of all lives. May you seize it, use it to
the full and create for yourselves and your
brothers a new life.

My people are preparing My Way. Make
yourselves one with them, help them, keep
close contact with their work and let them
show you the way.

My Plan runs smoothly.
My Purposes are being fulfilled.
My Rule is being approached.
My Time is near.
My Law will be established.
My Love is spread abroad.
My Teaching will show men the way forward,
the only way left to them,
the Way of Old,
the Way of God,
the Way of True Men, True Sons of God.

My Love will be established in the hearts
of men and together in Love we shall know
God, see the Face of Him Who sits on the
Shining Throne. Together we shall kneel
at His Feet and know the Peace of God.
That is My Task. Let Me take you there,
My friends and brothers. Respond quickly
to My Presence and Teaching and I may lead
you before the Throne.

Make haste, My friends, all is well, all
is fast being accomplished.
My Mission shall flourish.

May the Divine Light and Love and Power
of the One Most Holy God be now manifest
within your hearts and minds.
May this manifestation lead you to see that
you are but aspects of God.

Message No. 28

May 9th 1978

I am with you once more, My dear friends.

I would like to show you a new way to live, a way based on the innate brotherhood of Man, on his capacity to love and share, and on his essential divinity.

The process of becoming divine is a simple one, a natural one, open freely to all men. It is the process of releasing that God Who, from the beginning, has dwelt within you.
My Promise is this: if you will follow Me into the New Time, I shall release for you your divine nature.
I am the Way and the Means to God, for I guard the Gates through which all men pass to come to the feet of God.
If you can trust Me to show you the Way, I shall lead you forwards and upwards and take you to Him. That is My Task.

I tell you only what you already know: that men are brothers; but when that brotherhood becomes manifest in the world that divinity likewise shall shine forth.

My Emergence proceeds. Many now there are who know Me and call Me friend, who salute Me daily, whose smile of welcome I cherish. Soon I shall be known to you in a certain fashion, outlining for you the possibilities of change. May you quickly see Me, know Me and work for Me.

My Plan is to show Myself to the world so
soon now that there will remain but little
doubt that the Lord of Love is here,
that the Son of Man is among you,
that the Prince of Peace has returned.

May the Divine Light and Love and Power of
the One Most Holy God be now manifest
within your hearts and minds.
May this manifestation lead you to seek and
know that Divine Light within your heart
which is very God.

Message No. 29

May 16th 1978

My dear friends, I am happy to be with you
once more and to release to you a fragment
of My Teaching.

My Masters will teach you the Rules of Life,
I Myself will show you that higher Light
which beckons mankind.
My Teaching is twofold: it has to do with
Man's physical nature, the necessities of
life; it has to do, also, with Man's
relationship to that Divine Being Whom we
call God.
In My vocabulary these are as one, for only
in so far as Man correctly relates to Man
does he so relate to God. My Plan is to
show you this, to teach you that when Man
discovers in himself the ability to share,
to love, to trust, from that moment begins
his ascent to God.
It was always so and always shall be so.

My Coming has been expected by millions.
My Arrival among you is known to relatively
few. Nevertheless, these few can tell the
others and light in them the joy which My
Promise brings.

My Mission is now under way, achieving results.
Soon, in My Centre, My Face and Name will be
known and will attract to Me those who seek
to serve. May you be among them.

66

My precise abode is not so important. What
you should look for is My Message, My Call,
and respond from your heart.
My Task begins well and soon you shall see
the creation of a new map, of a New Country.
That Country I call Love.

May the Divine Light and Love and Power of
the One Most Holy God be now manifest within
your hearts and minds.
May this manifestation lead you to seek and
to find that Divine Spark which in truth you
are.

Message No. 30

May 23rd 1978

My dear friends, I am happy to be with you
once more.

My Plan runs smoothly; My work proceeds and
now in My Centre My Name and Face are known
to many. Your brothers seek My help and
bring to Me their troubles. I welcome this
and soon shall stand for them in greater
stead.

My Masters are working now to bring about
the transformation of your social life,
the old forms of which are rotten and
perished. Under Their guidance your brothers
are preparing the new forms, the new lines
of action, through which may be expressed
the new aspirations of Man in this New Age.

Allow Me to tell you this: My Mission is
proceeding so well now that soon the world
will know –
that the Forerunner has returned,
that the Way of Truth is open,
that the Light of the future beckons,
that the Cry of Man has been heard,
that the Plan of God works out,
that the Signs of the New can be seen,
that the Love of God shall be expressed.
My Coming is the guarantee of all of this.

I am the Answer to the past.
I am the Hope for the future.
I am the Lamp.
I am the Path to God.
I am the Secret One.
I am the Foundation.
I am the Presence.

Join your brothers in service to Me and to
the world. Prepare for My Emergence and
create a new and happier world for all men.
Do this now, My friends.
Prepare to see Me soon.
Prepare to acknowledge Me.
Prepare to sound the note of triumph of the
Truth.

May the Divine Light and Love and Power of
the Everlasting God be now manifest within
your hearts and minds. May this manifestation
lead you to be ever within the Aura of the
Living God.

Message No. 31

May 30th 1978

My dear friends, I am happy to be with you once
more.

My Plan proceeds well. I am among friends,
your brothers know Me and love Me and for
them shall I speak.

When you see Me you will know why I have come,
for I shall appeal to you in these terms:
Save My little ones; feed your brothers.
Remember that Mankind is One, children of
the One Father.
Make over, in trust, the goods of the Earth
to all who are in need.
Do this now and save the world.

Thus shall I speak; so shall be My Appeal;
and when Mankind has accepted this Law
I shall declare Myself.
Many there are now who know this to be true,
who desire to share, who long for brotherhood,
yet act not.
Nothing happens by itself. Man must act and
implement his will.
Today, that will is the will, also, of God.
Therefore, the outcome is assured.

My brothers, why wait for My Appearance?
Why sit still when the world groans; when men,
women and children die in misery, cast off
by their brothers?

There is no greater aspiration than the desire
to serve. Make your act of service the
saving of the starving of the world and help
My Plan.

My Army is arrayed, in position; the Light
of Truth shines in their eyes and at the Call
from Me it will act.
See yourselves as one of that Company of
Light and be assured that My Love will act
through you.
Make yourselves one of that joyous Company
and be assured of My Strength.
Take up the challenge which this service
presents and be fulfilled in this life.

My Mission is beginning but already the
wheels are turning, the Blueprint of Truth
descends and My Light shines in the hearts
of men.

May the Divine Light and Love and Power of
the One and Holy God be now manifest within
your hearts and minds. May this manifestation
lead you to be that Centre of Light which in
truth you are.

Message No. 32

June 13th 1978

My dear friends, I am with you once more.

My Appearance among men is nigh. Soon, for
yourselves, you will know that I am with you.
Your brothers, already, know Me and trust
Me and look to Me as leader. In this fashion
shall I speak for them and to the world,
placing before Mankind the choices.
Many hear Me even now, listen to My words,
and ponder, for I tell them what in their
hearts they know.
I tell them that Justice is a Law of God.
I tell them that Love is the Way to the
Source.
I show them that without Love and Justice
Mankind will perish.
My brothers love Me for these Truths, for
they recognise them to stand behind all life.
Thus shall I speak and thus shall you know
that I am among you. Make haste to follow
Me, to create the New Time, the glorious
future which shines ahead for Mankind.

Let Me speak to you simply My friends.
Let Me trace for you the Plan of God for that
future.
Let Me show you the way to manifest that God
which you are, and so complete that Plan.

Perhaps you are surprised by the fact of My
early return, but men and women weep, children
die, and others laugh in blind forgetfulness.

My Coming is not by chance but by Law and Love.
That Law and that Love have brought Me here.
When you see Me you will see a friend and brother, and I shall know My Coming has not been in vain.

May the Divine Light and Love and Power of the One Most Holy God be now manifest within your hearts and minds.
May this manifestation lead you to see your true nature as Love.

Message No. 33

June 22nd 1978

My dear friends, I am happy to be with you once more.

Many will see Me soon, will harken to My words, and follow My lead.
May you be among the first to do so for in this way you can become My Co-workers. My need for such is great.
Many there are who share My hope for the restoration of our world. Seek them out and work with them. Build together a stronghold of Light and illumine the path for your brothers.
Sit not still, but act, and restore the Time of Truth.
My Masters will point the path for you and under Their guidance you can create great achievements.

My purpose tonight is to tell you that My methods are simple indeed. My Plan is this:
To place before mankind the alternatives of sharing and death.
No-one in Truth could for mankind choose the latter, for that death would be shameful and bitter indeed, unlike your blackest fears.
My friends, there is a way of Hope. There is a way into the Light. That simple way lies through brotherhood and love.
Many times before have you heard this.
Nevertheless, mankind yet awaits its fulfilment.

Make then, gladly, your choice for Life, for
Justice and Sharing, and follow Me into your
most glorious and shining future.
Make this your choice, My friends, and be
endowered with your true stature as very Gods.

May the Divine Light and Love and Power of
the One Most Holy God be now manifest within
your hearts and minds.
May this manifestation lead you to seek and
to find that Centre of Silence within you all.

Message No. 34

June 29th 1978

My dear friends, I am with you once more and
am happy to speak to you in this way.

I am with you in a very real sense, but soon
you will see Me more clearly and, when you do,
you will see your Friend and Elder Brother.
My Mission proceeds rhythmically and well and
My Plans are, without doubt, receiving due
response from mankind.
Many there are now who heed Me without the
knowledge of My Presence, but the hearts of
men respond and soon a great transformation
will take place in the world.
Many are sensing My Presence, however obliquely,
and heeding My Call.
Through them I work, through them My Plan
works out.

When I make My Declaration before mankind
many will realise that in their hearts they
saw Me.
When that day comes I shall look upon you all,
brothers and sisters, as workers for the
Light and engage you in the transforming of
our world.

When I announce Myself to the world I shall
speak to all men in these terms:
Prepare to see yourselves as Gods.
Prepare to be uplifted into Light.
Prepare to realise yourselves as brothers,
one of another.

Prepare to teach the Truth.
Prepare to live the Law.
Welcome this Law and restore the Plan of God.

May the Divine Light and Love and Power of
the One Most Holy God be now manifest within
your hearts and minds.
May this manifestation lead you to seek and
to find that Essence of Truth which forever
you have been.

Message No. 35

July 6th 1978

My dear friends, I am happy to be with you
once more.

My Plans work out. My Emergence takes a
little time but proceeds well. Soon, among
your brothers, My Teaching will begin and,
resounding through the world, will usher in
a New Age.

My Promise holds: I shall take before the
Throne of God all who can follow Me into the
Higher Light which I bring. May you be among
those who shall know this joy.
Take your place by My side and together shall
we make all things new.
Take My hand, My friends, and let Me guide
you through My Garden.
Let Me show you My Flowers.
Let Me teach you My Law.

My Heart enfolds you as always and on each
step of the upward path My Hand steadies
and guides.
I am your Master, Brother and Friend. Know
Me then in this way.
Let Me teach you the simple Path to God.
Let Me show you the Greater Light Divine.
Let us travel together this Path
and know the Secrets of Old,
know the Wonders of God,
know the Blessing of Love.

The cry for Justice from men has reached My
ears and to that cry I hearken.
The call for succour has risen to Me and I
hasten to give.
The pain of the world sits heavily on My
heart and this gladly would I lighten.
My Pain can be yours; My Burden can be
shared. I offer you both.
Take My Pain, My brothers, and turn it into
Joy.
Ease My Burden, My friends, and know Bliss.

May the Divine Light and Love and Power of
the One Most Holy God be now manifest within
your hearts and minds.
May this manifestation lead you to see that
you are always and ever Centres in the Being
of God.

Message No. 36

July 13th 1978

I am with you once more, My dear friends.

All is well. My planned Emergence is taking
place and within a short time, in My Centre,
My Face will be known.
The first phase has been successfully completed
and in Joy may you await My Teaching.
When you see Me you will know that the time
has come for change.
The world awaits the sounding of the Cosmic
Dates.
The nations prepare for a New Dispensation
and in Trust and Brotherhood all men will
share.

My Masters are now emerging more quickly
than planned; this stimulus will bring great
benefits to the world, conveying as They do
the Love of God.
My Masters will help you to manifest this
Divine Love, will show you the simple Way of
Truth, the Blessing of Trust.

Be not afraid, My friends, for all will be well.
The New Light shines, the New Country beckons,
and in that Country I shall show you the Wonders
of God.
Be ready to follow Me therein and be enabled
to manifest your God-given greatness.

May the Divine Light and Love and Power of the
One Most Holy God be now manifest within your
hearts and minds.
May this manifestation lead you to be ever
enfolded in the indwelling Light and Love of
God.

Message No. 37

July 18th 1978

My dear friends, I am pleased indeed to speak
to you once more.

My Mission goes well. My heart fills with joy
at the prospect of My renewed contact with My
brothers.
All who love and serve their brothers I think
of in this way.

My immediate Plan is to reveal Myself stage
by stage in a certain fashion, and, broadening
My field of work, speak for all men.
Soon I shall be among you in a way unmistakable
to your prepared hearts.
By this means will you know Me:
by My Light which shines through you, awakening
you to service and Love.
By this means will you know Me:
by My Call for Justice and Reason.
By this means shall you know Me:
by My work among your brothers, those who need
My help.
My Appeal shall sound forth - save the world,
help those who suffer and die in need.
My Call shall resound - correct the mistakes
of the past and renew the Spirit of Man; make
way for Love in your hearts and see God.
Thus shall I speak, My friends, and thus will
you know Me.

My task begins, a task which for long have I
planned in wisdom and joy, a task which for Me
is the fulfilment of My Mission and the fulfilment
of the Will of God.

May the Divine Light and Love and Power of the
One Most Holy God be now manifest within your
hearts and minds.
May this manifestation lead you to be ever
mindful of your true Splendour as Sparks of God.

Message No. 38

July 25th 1978

I am with you once more, My dear friends.

I am happy to be able to tell you that there
are those among your brothers who have seen Me
and have given Me their allegiance. They
trust Me to show them the forward path, that
path which leads upwards into the Light of
God.
Let Me take you with Me into that Divine
Light, to show you the marvels which await
your astonished eyes.
My dear children, I would like to show you
that to love God and to love Man are the same;
as we love our brothers so do we manifest our
love of God.
Theoretically you know this, but, My dear
friends, the practice of love is essential, for
by Love alone will this Earth be sustained.

My efforts are proving successful in changing
the balance in the world. Men are ready to
receive Me; knowingly or not they await My
Presence. Daily I hearken to their prayers.

My Masters are among you in a new way,
closer to you than ever before, sowing the
seeds of Love and Trust among the nations.
May it be that these seeds of Love will find
fertile soil.

My Plan is to emerge forthwith, to speak to
the people simply and in language which all
men may understand; to speak to them as
brothers, to guide their footsteps in the
direction of God.
God may be known by many names: I call Him
Love; I call Him also Justice.
Both Love and Justice are the foundation of
our life.
Seek Me out and know your Brother of Old.
Hearken to My Message, My friends, and together
in joy shall we transform this world.

May the Divine Light and Love and Power of
the One Most Holy God be now manifest within
your hearts and minds.
May this manifestation lead you to be ever
enfolded in the ever-flowing Blessing and Love
of God.

Message No. 39

August 1st 1978

My dear friends, I am with you once more, and
happy I am to be so.

My Teaching goes forth. My words resound on
all planes, and act to bring Light to Mankind.
Soon, in My Centre, men will awake to find among
them the Son of Man, for, My friends, My
Mission proceeds and My Steps are sounding the
New Time.
Your brothers know Me, accept Me for one of
themselves and make Me at home in the world.
When you see Me you will find a Brother and
Friend, a Teacher and Guide, a Refuge and Shield.
Look for My Emergence soon and be prepared to work
for Me, to show your brothers the way forward,
the way into the Light, the way to know the
Secrets of God.

To show you these have I come.
To teach you the simple Truths am I here.
To lead you into the Blessed Country of Love
have I returned.
Make it your task to find Me quickly, to light
the lamp of your brother, to send My Words into
the world to reach your brother's heart.
May you be among those who quickly find and
recognise Me, for, if you do, you may become
My Warriors.

My Task begins. It is a task for which I have
waited long, but one which I shoulder with joy.
My Army is now on the move and soon the clash
of battle will be heard.
The outcome of this battle is assured, for at
My side are True Sons of God.
Take your places in the ranks of My Army, My
friends, and create the New Time, the Time of
God.

May the Divine Light and Love and Power of
the One Most Holy God be now manifest within
your hearts and minds.
May this manifestation lead you to be ever
mindful that you are, now and forever, Children
of God.

Message No. 40

August 8th 1978

My dear friends, I am happy to be with you once
more.

I shall soon be known to you in more complete
fashion and you will know for yourselves that
I am among you.

My Love is changing the world. Today, men
stand ready for a new life, a new Principle,
the Principle of Love.
That is My gift to you.

My Army is ready for battle, My Masters of
Wisdom and Myself at the head.
That battle will be fought for the continuance
of Man on this Earth.
Rest assured that My Army shall triumph.

My Law will be accepted by men.
My Love will blossom in their hearts, and
through this Law of Love Mankind will know
God.
My Teaching will show you the way to God, the
simple path of Justice and Love.
My Masters will teach you the ancient Laws
and Lore, and bring you before Me.

I am the Light.
I am the Law.
I am the Ascended One.
I am the knower of God's Will.
I am the Beacon.
I am the Support of all men.

I know men's hearts and seek to purify them.
I know men's cares and seek to help them.
I know the anguish of many and return to save
them.

My brothers and friends, I am with you and
around you.
I am your loving heart.
I am your highest thought.
I am your pity.

Manifest that which I am and know the bliss
which comes to those who know God.

May the Divine Light and Love and Power of the
One Most Holy God be now manifest within your
hearts and minds.
May this manifestation lead you into the Arms
of the Everlasting God.

Message No. 41

September 7th 1978

My dear friends, I am happy to be with you once
more.

You shall see Me soon, and when you do, without
doubt you will know that your Brother, Maitreya
Himself, is among you.

I am with you in many ways, chief among these
as the Embodiment of Love.
This Principle of Love underlies all Being,
and without its manifestation, Life would
cease to be.
My Mission is to evoke the Principle of Love
in all men, and for those who are ready, to
show a Higher Truth.

The means are simple:
Through Justice and Freedom for all, that Love
can be expressed.
Through the manifestation of man's Brotherhood,
the Source of All can be known.
May it be that you will quickly see this,
understand the purpose of life and show the way
for your brothers.
Thus can you take part in the transformation of
your world.

My Masters are developing, through Their groups,
new forms and structures for your life.
These will allow you better to express the
Divine Beings which you are, and thus complete
the Plan.

Take part, My friends, in this great adventure
of Spirit, and allow Me to show you, and lead
you into, your heritage.

May the Divine Light and Love and Power of the
One Most Holy God be now manifest within your
hearts and minds.
May this manifestation bring you swiftly and
surely to the feet of God.

My dear friends, I am happy to be with you
once more.

Many times have you heard Me say that My
Coming means change.
Specifically, the greatest change will be in
the hearts and minds of men, for My Return
among you is a sign that men are ready to
receive new life.
That New Life for men do I bring in abundance.
On all the planes this Life will flow, reaching
the hearts and souls and bodies of men, bringing
them nearer to the Source of Life Itself.
My task will be to channel those Waters of Life
through you.

I am the Water Carrier.
I am the Vessel of Truth.
That Truth shall I reveal to you and lift you
into your true nature.

I am the River.
Through Me flows the new stream of God-given
life, and this shall I bestow on you.
Thus shall we together walk through My Garden,
smell the perfume of My Flowers, and know the
joy of closeness to God.

My friends, these things are not dreams.
All of this will be yours.
My Mission will vouchsafe this to you.

May the Divine Light and Love and Power of the
One Most Holy God be now manifest within your
hearts and minds.
May this manifestation take you into the Lap of
the Everlasting God.

Message No. 43

September 19th 1978

My dear friends, I am happy to be with you once
more.

My Pledge will be fulfilled.
I shall take before the Shining One all who
can follow Me into the Higher Light, and in
this way shall you see the Face of God.

My friends, God is nearer to you than you can
imagine.
God is yourself.
God is within you and all around you.
God also sits in majesty on the Golden Throne,
and when you are ready, we shall kneel together
at His Divine Feet.
Thus shall it be.
Make haste to follow Me therefore, to reach the
heights from which can be seen the Glories of
God, the Blessed Country of Love, the River of
Truth.
Allow Me to take you with Me into that fair land
and show you the wonders of your inheritance.

My Masters are training Their groups to show
the way to implement man's needs.
Through this manifestation all goodness will
follow.
My Masters know the problems which beset man
today; the answers likewise are in Their grasp.
Allow Them to lead, My friends, and show you the
simple path of Joy, Simplicity and Truth.

A new Law descends.
A new Truth becomes known to man.
The Law is Love.
The Truth, My friends, is Brotherhood.
My Mission will ensure that that Law and that
Truth shall become manifest.
This I promise you and thus shall it be.

May the Divine Light and Love and Power of
the One Most Holy God be now manifest within
your hearts and minds.
May this manifestation lead you to be ever
enfolded by the Living God.

Message No. 44

September 26th 1978

My dear friends, I am happy to be with you once
again, and to tell you that My Emergence
proceeds well.

My Face is known to a growing number of your
brothers, but My Name for the present must
remain undisclosed. In this way, My Secret
can be maintained.
Why should this be so?
To enable you, My friends and brothers, to find
Me from the Light within you, that Light which
I bring.
You must know and want that for which I stand;
within your hearts must burn the desire for
Justice and Truth.
Where these Divine Aspects are present you will
recognise Me. I envisage little difficulty for
those who follow My Law, for this Law evokes
within you the desire for Truth.

My Presence is causing such changes in the
world that before long the knowledge of My
existance will be ascertained.
Men will raise the question: how can it be;
from where does this new light shine?
The divisions of old will merge and grow
together; the sons of men will sense a higher
Light and, turning their faces towards that
Light, shall find Me waiting to lead them.
Thus shall it be. Thus shall the Truth in the
hearts of men respond to the Truth which I am.
Thus shall that New Light be kindled in their
hearts, and the anguish of men depart.

This time, My friends, is near.
This time, My brothers, is almost upon you.
Wake to the fact of My Presence!
Wake to the promise of your deliverance!

May the Divine Light and Love and Power of the
One Most Holy God be now manifest within your
hearts and minds.
May this manifestation lead you out of
ignorance into the Light.

Message No. 45

October 3rd 1978

My dear friends, I am happy indeed to be with
you once again and to speak to you in this way.

My Presence is being felt throughout the world.
My energy of Love, My Gift, creates among men
a pool of happiness.
Dip deeply therein, My friends, and, shining
with the Light of Love, emerge into a New Day.

My Masters are working to trace for you the
outlines of the future.
Bear these well in mind. The rock upon which
that glorious future will be built is Love,
Justice and Sharing.
Make it your aim, My friends, to link yourselves
with those for whom these Aspects are Divine.
Create between you a wall of Light against
which the world will knock in vain.

My Army moves.
My lieutenants know the result of the battle
and know the Plan of action.
That action involves you all, for through you,
My friends and brothers, must the New World be
made.
Take then your part in this valiant work and
show your mettle.
My Love will sustain you.
My Law will guide you.
My Heart enfolds you always.
My friends, be not afraid - you have nothing
to fear but your fear.

May the Divine Light and Love and Power of the
One Most Holy God be now manifest within your
hearts and minds.
May this manifestation lead you into the battle,
and, with your brothers, to victory.

Message No. 46

October 10th 1978

My dear friends, I am happy to be with you once
more.
My friends, I am happy, too, to tell you that
My Work proceeds to plan. All goes well and
soon My Face and Voice shall become known to
you.
May this manifestation release in you that
aspiration which I know shines ever in your
heart.
May it be that you will accept Me and work
closely with Me for your brothers.
My major need today is for those who share My
Vision to accept the responsibility of action.
Many millions there are in the world who know
the need of man, who see that Vision, but
know not the urgency of the time.
I rely on all those with a knowledge of your
brothers' needs, a sympathy for the sufferings
of so many and a will to change all that.
May you be among those upon whom I may call,
that together we can usher in a new and better
world.

My heart responds to the tremor of your
aspiration.
My Love kindles that fire.
My friends, fan that into a blaze and come with
Me.
Hold fast to your vision of what may be and
reveal the God within you all.

May the Divine Light and Love and Power of the One Most Holy God be now manifest within your hearts and minds.
May this manifestation lead you to be ever mindful of your identity with God.

Message No. 47

October 24th 1978

My dear friends, once again I am with you and
happy I am to be so.

Many are the ways in which you may recognise
Me.
Look for Me, My friends, as a Teacher of men,
outlining the possibilities of the New Time.
Remember that I am a man among men as well as
a True Son of God.
My Masters, too, are simple men and come to
live among you as such.
Nothing separates Us from you; we shall live
and work among you as brothers.
Remember this and look not for Gods.

My Teachings will be simple indeed, will show
you the way to God through Love and Service to
man.
My Plans are proceeding well and soon My Face
will become known to you.
May it be that you will allow Me to guide you
into the future.

Very many now await My Presence.
Throughout the world men stand ready and poised
for My Appearance, knowingly or not.
When enough are so prepared My Teaching will
penetrate their hearts and in Joy and Love will
they follow Me.
My heart knows this and makes light My Task.

May you be among the first of those who draw
around Me, through whom I may work and who in
this way can best serve their brothers.
My love for you knows no end.

May the Divine Light and Love and Power of the
One Most Holy God be now manifest within your
hearts and minds.
May this manifestation lead you to be
enlightened from your own True Self.

Message No. 48

October 31st 1978

I am with you once more, My dear friends.

It is part of My Plan to reveal Myself
gradually, step by step to make My Presence
known to the world.
This process is now well under way.
When you see Me you will find a Friend in need,
a Brother Whose heart enfolds your own, a
Teacher Who has travelled somewhat further
along the journey of life, a Guide into that
blessed future which, My friends, will be yours.

My methods, simple as they are, are proving
effective.
Witness for yourselves the changes occuring in
the world.

My entreaty is this: make yourself responsible
for the spreading of the news of My Presence
and do for Me a great work.
When your brothers know that I am with you
they will gladly accept your news.
Do this for Me My friends.
Do this now.
Share with your brothers and sisters everywhere
this message of hope, these tidings of joy,
and prepare them, too, for My Appearance.
In this way you can serve your brothers beyond
measure.

I am taking you into a New Country.
Close your ranks around Me and allow Me to show
you the glories which await you.
The framework of this future time is now
constructed.
The blueprint of the future becomes clearer.
Let Me take you with Me into that future and
clothe in radiant Light that structure.
My Blessings go with you all.

May the Divine Light and Love and Power of
the One Most Holy God be now manifest within
your hearts and minds.
May this manifestation lead you to see yourselves
as the Divine and glorious Beings that you are.

Message No. 49

November 7th 1978

My dear friends, I am happy indeed to be with
you once more and to tell you that My Face
will soon be known.

Your brothers support Me, give Me their trust
and their love, a love which I cherish.
So shall it be with you, My friends, when we
meet together.

Soon you will see the manifestation of a
great change in the world. That change is
wrought by My Energies and Presence.
Have no fear, all is well and proceeds to plan.

My Brothers, the Masters of Wisdom, will lead
you forward into the light of that Wisdom which
is Theirs, will unfold for you the panorama of
man's past, will teach you the ancient Laws
and guide your feet into the future.
Look to Them as to an elder brother and, trusting,
let Them show you the Lighted Way.

My Plans unfold.
My Heart embraces all who know Me, who come to
Me for help.
Thus shall it always be.
My brothers and sisters, My help is yours to
command, you have only to ask.
Take My Hand, My friends, and let Me take you
with Me into your Glory.

My Mission begins. Already, much is accomplished.
Soon the tide will turn and men will sense and
respond in joy to My Presence.
Make it your task to tell the others that I am
among you.
Lead them, too, into the Light.
Allow them to share with you this realisation
and give to them the hope they need.
In this way, My friends, you will serve Me more
than you could know.

May the Divine Light and Love and Power of the
One Most Holy God be now manifest within your
hearts and minds.
May this manifestation bring you into the
realisation of your true nature as Messengers of
God.

My dear friends, I am happy indeed to be with
you once more.

My Mission proceeds, My Plans evolve correctly.
Very little time now will elapse until you see
My Face.
Know it as the face of your Friend and Brother,
come once again to help you.
Take Me to your hearts as I, My dear brothers
and sisters, have taken you to Mine, and,
working together, let us remake the world.
Let us change all that is corrupt and useless
in your structures, all that prevents the
manifestation of your Divinity.
Let us together show the way for the little
ones and hold fast the world for them.
I appeal to you to aid Me in My Task of succour.
Help Me to help the world, and fulfil this
life.

My Coming is planned, is lawful and releases to
you the Love and Will of God.
I am the Manifestation of both Love and Will.
I am the Caretaker.
I am the One sent to teach you.
I am the Flute Player.

Many times before have I been among you.
Many times before have you given Me your love.
Once again, My friends, demonstrate your
allegiance and work with Me.

I am the Lawgiver.
I hear all pleas.
I come to Save.
I render Service.

Make yourselves one with Me and let us together
serve the Plan.

My Masters, too, are with you. Let Them guide
you into the future.
Make haste to serve Me.
Your brothers call both Me and you.
My people heed Me. Join them, and manifest
that which I am through you.

May the Divine Light and Love and Power of the
One Most Holy God be now manifest within your
hearts and minds.
May this Light and Love and Power lead to the
manifestation of that Divine Being Whom in
truth you are.

Message No. 51

November 23rd 1978

My dear friends, I am with you once more.

My Mission, as I have said, is twofold: to
release you from the bondage of your self-
imposed limitations, and to take you with
Me back to God.
I shall show you that through the right
distribution of this earth's manifold resources
all men may enjoy God's bounty.
I shall show you, too, that the Path to God
is simple indeed, that your Divine Spark will
become manifest through Me.

Let Me do this work for you, My friends.
Let Me lead you into your Divine Heritage.
I shall show you wonders of which you cannot
dream.
I shall release from your eyes the blindfold
of ignorance.
I shall drive from this earth forever the
curse of hatred, the sin of separation.
Let Me take you with Me, My friends, back to
your Source, back to the cradle of your Being,
and release in you your Godhead.

My Masters will serve you, too, will teach you
to live together in true brotherhood, in
justice and harmony.
Forget not, My brothers, that you are One,
that the Father of All has created you in His
Divine Image, that through you shines the
same blessed Light of Love and Truth.

The time is coming, My friends, when the Light of Truth shall shine all around you, when Man shall take his brother to his heart and know him as himself.
Let Me lead you, My friends, into that blessed state.
Say yes to My Advent.
Say yea to My Coming, and be enfolded in the blessing of My Love.

May the Divine Light and Love and Power of the One Most Holy God be now manifest within your hearts and minds.
May this manifestation lead you to see yourselves, together, as children of the One Father.

Message No. 52

November 28th 1978

My dear friends, I am happy to be with you
once more.

My Plans are achieving their effects, and
many stand today in wonder at the changes
which arise.
Thus, quietly, do I affect the balance of
the world.
My energies of Love and Will create a reservoir
of Truth from which all men may drink.
Keep open your heart to this Higher Stream and
make yourself a channel for Me. I need many
such.

The problems of mankind are real but solvable.
The solution lies within your grasp.
Take your brother's need as the measure for
your action and solve the problems of the
world.
There is no other course.

Mankind today faces a dilemma of Truth - to
march with Me into the future or forever to
despair.
Place yourselves behind Me in My Task and
allow Me to take you on the Lighted Way.
My Masters will help you, and together in
Freedom and Trust shall all men receive the
Blessings of God.

My Plans unfold, and soon, in full and physical
fact, shall you know Me and, trusting, follow
Me.
Be not surprised if My words are familiar to
you; many times before have you heard the need
for Love.
Nevertheless, many today stand naked of this
Divine Aspect and perish in millions.
Therefore, My friends, My words will resound
in your ears:
Love your brother; heed his need; give of your
plenty and restore joy to the world.

May the Divine Light and Love and Power of the
One Most Holy God be now manifest within your
hearts and minds.
May this manifestation lead you to be ever
mindful of your identity with your brothers
and God.

Message No. 53

December 7th 1978

My dear friends, I am happy to be with you
once more.

My methods meet with success. My agents
work correctly and well, and all proceeds
to plan.
My Plan is to remain in My Centre until My
Declaration is made.
Then My Progression round the countries of
the world will begin, and all men shall see
My Face.
When I place Myself before you I shall ask
for your allegiance, for your help in service
to your brothers.
I know already those on whom I may count.

My task will be to take you on a journey into
Truth, into the Blessed Country of Love, and
there to show you to yourselves as God.
My Masters, likewise, will take you by the
hand and lead you to His Divine Feet.

Let us together show the world:
that the need for war is past;
that the instinct of man is to live and to
love;
that hatred is begotten of separation;
that the Law of God lives in man and is
fundamental to his nature.
All of this shall I show you. Work with Me
and prove this to be true.

I am the Conveyor of God's Love.
I am the Administrator of God's Will.
The Light of God dwells in Me and that Light
do I turn on you.
Grow therein, My friends, and shine with the
Glory of God.

My Plan is to reveal Myself in such a way
that few, indeed, will know not who I am.
Therefore, watch for My Presence.
Seek out My Face and Words and hearken quickly
to them.

My Blessing goes with you all.

May the Divine Light and Love and Power of the
One Most Holy God be now manifest within your
hearts and minds.
May this manifestation lead you to be ever
mindful of your likeness to God.

Message No. 54

December 14th 1978

My dear friends, I am happy to be with you
once more and to share with you My thoughts
for man's future.

Man has far to go, for man stems from the
highest source.
Within all men sits a God. That God is
your true Self.
My Task will be to release in you that
Divine Being, and so complete a Divine Plan.

There is nothing more simple than God, for
behind all things rests that Divine Principle.
When man sees this he will come into his
true greatness, and from him then will flow
a creative stream.
My Plan is to show you, step by step, the way
to manifest that Divine Principle and thus
lead you to your Source.
If men accept Me they shall come into the
Truth of their Godhead, and in the shining
raiment of that Truth shall stand revealed
as God.
That promise I do solemnly make.

Help Me. My friends, to do this work for you.
Reveal, now, the Spirit of God which already
shines within you, and together in Truth let
us remake this world.

116

May the Divine Light and Love and Power of
the One Most Holy God be now manifest within
your hearts and minds.
May this manifestation lead you to stand
revealed as the Gods you are.

Message No. 55

December 19th 1978

My dear friends, I am happy to be with you once more and to add My glad tidings to this joyous festival.

My friends, I am with you here tonight in a certain fashion, but soon you shall become aware that I, Maitreya Himself, your Eldest Brother, am among you.
When you see Me you shall know that the turning point has been reached, that My Forces are gathered in strength, and that victory is assured.

My Plan is to release into the world My simple Teaching of Truth:
that men are one, brothers all;
that God loves all men equally;
that nature provides the sustenance for everyone to share;
that, coming as I do from mankind's past, I know the answers to man's dilemma.
I shall show you the simple ways of change, of correctly relating one to another, of correctly manifesting the Will of God.

My Plan is to show you this and release you from your limitations.
The way ahead is not easy, My friends, but with your help all shall be made good for mankind.

Take heart, My dear friends, from these words,
and be assured of my help and strength.

May the Divine Light and Love and Power of
the One Most Holy God be now manifest within
your hearts and minds.
May this manifestation lead you to sense the
need of your brother, and, sensing that, to
render service to him.

Message No. 56

January 9th 1979

My dear friends, I am happy to be close to you
once more.

My friends, I am with you today in such a way,
to remind you of My Presence, and also of your
task in the weeks and months ahead.
Many there are now in every corner of the world
who sense that I am here; who study events and
draw conclusions; who see the changes which
daily mount in potency, and read the signs
manifest in the world.
But many still are blind to the reality of
My Presence among you, and this state would I
gladly have you remedy.
Teach your brothers the truth of My Coming,
the truth of My Departure so long ago, and
the Promise which I now bring.
Tell them that Maitreya, their Brother, the
Eldest of such, is with them once more.
Tell them that soon, for themselves, they
will see Me and hear My Words, and rejoice in
My Presence.
Tell them that I come to teach the simple Laws
of God, to teach men to share, to lead them
into the Light of Truth, and to establish among
them a vast network of Divine Light.

You, My friends, can aid Me in this task.
Take your place at My side. Lead your brothers
into that Light, and show that for men exists
a future bedecked in the Glory of God, a
future vouchsafed to all men.

120

Tell your brothers this, My friends, and make
way in their hearts for My Light and Love.
Prepare the ground before My Feet.
Sustain My Task, and help yourselves to Bliss.

May the Divine Light and Love and Power of the
One Most Holy God be now manifest within your
hearts and minds.
May this manifestation lead you to be ever
open to the influence of the Agents of God.

Message No. 57

January 16th 1979

My dear friends, I am happy to be with you
once more.

With the year 1979 begins a new phase of
mankind's life.
My Presence is producing such changes that
no one but the most blind will, shortly,
deny My existence among you.

My work proceeds smoothly and well, and all
aspects of My Plan are being fulfilled.
Nevertheless, there still is much to do, and
I would set you, therefore, this task:
Tell men everywhere that you believe that the
Teacher for mankind is among them.
Tell them what you know of My plans and
projects, and illumine their lives.
Send My Words throughout the world and reach
the hearts of your brothers.
Help them, too, to share in a great manifestation
of God's Love, and awaken them to the promise
of the future.
Do this for Me, My friends, and you will do
a deed of which forever you may be proud.

The central point of My Plan is to evoke in
men the desire to share, for on this Principle,
all else rests.

Sharing, My friends, is an attribute of God.
To become the Gods which you are, this
Principle must govern your lives.
Allow Me to remind you of this simple truth
once again, and show you the path to the
future.
My Blessing goes with you all.

May the Divine Light and Love and Power of the
One Most Holy God be now manifest within your
hearts and minds.
May this manifestation allow you to teach the
Truth to all you meet.

Message No. 58

January 23rd 1979

My dear friends, I am happy indeed to be with
you once more.

My Law is beginning to be fulfilled.
The ways of Man are changing.
This I see more clearly, perhaps, than you can,
but, if you will believe Me, it is so.

All that I say tonight pertains to the creation
of a new living structure for mankind.
A new civilisation must be built on the ruins
of the old.
That which is precious and worth preserving will
be so preserved, but all that hinders the
manifestation of Man's true greatness must be
discarded.
A time is coming, My friends, when you will see
around you cities of beauty, glowing creations
of Love, and all the manifestation of Man's
dreams of himself as God.
Thus will it be.

Many are the ways to perfection, but the simple
ways are best.
My Way, the Way of Love, will take Man quickest
to his Source.
If you can see this, you will proceed on a
Path unerring and true, and for all men this
is so.

124

When you see Me, you will know that the time
has come to begin this work of change, of
building the new, creating forms and structures
which will reveal yourselves to each other as
the Gods you are.
My Masters will help you in this work and I
shall lead.

My Plan is that you should see Me soon.
With your help this may be so.
I require the creation of a certain trust,
an expectancy and hope.
In this way no force need be used. My Law
forbids such force.
Therefore, My friends, the task is yours to
grasp.
Make known the fact that I am among you and
create the climate in which shortly I may be
seen.
That will not be as difficult as you might think,
for mankind today stands on the verge of a
revelation of its true nature and worth.
My Presence among you makes this so.
Your brothers will thank you for the work you do.

My Blessing goes with you all.

May the Divine Light and Love and Power of the
One Most Holy God be now manifest within your
hearts and minds.
May this manifestation lead you into the true
sense of yourselves as My Messengers.

Message No. 59

My brothers and sisters, happy I am to be
among you once more, and to reveal to you
My intentions and plans.

My dear friends, I am about to appear among
men in an altogether new and more potent
guise.
Many who see Me now wonder in their hearts
from whence I come.
Many see in Me their hopes and dreams fulfilled.
My Love penetrates their hearts and joyfully
they give Me their allegiance.
On a wider scale, also, will this be true, for,
when men see Me as I am, they will love Me and
hearken to My Words.
Have no fear, men will follow me for the love
in their hearts for their brothers, for it is
for all men everywhere that I shall speak.

Know Me by the simplicity of My utterance.
Know Me by the Love of My Heart,
by My deeds of succour,
by My call to all men to share and live in
peace.
Know Me thus, My friends, and give Me your
help.
I need not only your faith, but your willingness
to work for the unfoldment of God's Plan.
That Holy Plan shall I unfold for you, and
together in Love shall we see it fulfilled.

My Plan is to come before the world so quickly
now that nothing which prevents your
participation in this work should be allowed
to hinder.
Make it your primary task to acquaint your
brothers and sisters throughout the world with
the fact of My Presence, and create in them
the joy you know.
My Task will be to speak as the mouthpiece for
all men everywhere;
to voice for them their hopes and desires for
a better and saner life;
for the re-organisation of those structures
which prevent the manifestation of the true
divinity of man.

That is My Task, My dear friends, and that
Task lightly, and gladly, do I shoulder.
With your help it will be achieved.
Goodnight My dear friends.

May the Divine Light and Love and Power of the
One Most Holy God be now manifest within each
and every one whose inner Light I now see.

Message No. 60

February 6th 1979

My dear friends, I am happy to be among you
once more in this fashion.

My dear ones, My entreaty is this:
Make known the fact of My Presence among men
and become responsible for the speed of My
Emergence.
My Task is to take you through the Gates of
Initiation, to lead you upward to the Light
and back to the Source from which you come.
My intention is to proceed at once on My way,
to bring you, those who are ready, before the
Father, and to show you His Face.

I would have you know that much depends on you,
depends on your ability to create the necessary
hope and expectation for My Appearance.
I rely on you to do this work for Me and so
serve your brothers and Me.

I came before as a man misunderstood and rejected
by many.
I return today, not to conquer but to lead;
to show men their true nature as Sons of God;
to show men that they have come from a high
place, indeed, and thus have far to go.

I am the Means and the Way.
I am the Fruit of God's Labours.
I build the Temple of Love.
I accept those who are ready.
I love all men.

Take that which I am into your Being and reveal
the God Within.

I know God's Plan.
I teach all men.
I reveal the Truth.
I bring a New Light.
I create the New World through men.
I am the Beginning and the End.
I am the Love of God.
I am the Soul of Creation.
I am God made Flesh.
I am All Things.

I am your Heart.
I am your Delight.
I am your Purpose.
I am vouchsafed to you.

May the Divine Light and Love and Power of the
One Most Holy God be now manifest within your
hearts and minds.
May this manifestation clear from your eyes
the blindfold of ignorance.

Message No. 61

February 14th 1979

My dear friends, I am happy indeed to be among
you once more in this way, and to release to
you something of My Plans.

Within the group wherein I dwell are those
who know Me for what I am, but it is My
intention to withhold for a certain time My
true status.
This will enable you to see Me as one of
yourselves, a man among men.
Nothing which I do will seem extraordinary.
Nothing which I say will be bizarre or strange.
Simple indeed will be My approach. On this
fact you may count.

As a brother among brothers I shall speak for
you all, voice aloud your aspirations and
hopes;
make known the desire of all men for a world
at peace;
for a just and noble readiness to share;
for the creation of a society based on freedom
and love.
By My enunciation of these principles will you
know and discover Me.

My intention is to reveal Myself soon and by
the shortest route.
All else failing, I shall emerge into a world
ready but unprepared; a world which knows not
yet that I am among you.

But far better would it be for Me to come
before you as the Expected One, the One sent
by God to lead you into your future glory.
Many know this, but many more by far are
ignorant of the true happenings of the time.

I do solemnly appeal to you, therefore, My
dear friends, to make known the fact of My
Presence among you and pave smooth My Way.

My burdens are heavy indeed.
These burdens may be lightened by your work.
I trust you to act and follow.
Together we shall complete the Plan.

My Blessings go with you all.

May the Divine Light and Love and Power of
the One Most Holy God be now manifest within
your hearts and minds.
May this manifestation lead you to be ever
mindful of your true purpose as servants of
the Plan.

Message No. 62

February 21st 1979

My dear friends, I am happy indeed to be among
you once more.

My happy ones, My glad ones, I see within you
now the glow of the Light of Truth, the Truth
of My Presence among you.
That Light shall I fan into a blaze of glory
in this coming blessed time.

My Masters, too, are among you and will show
you the way to manifest your divine gifts, those
which lie dormant within your hearts.
My friends, I am nearer to you than you could
know, for I sit within the heart of all those
who love their brothers, of all those who wish
to share and release the light of Justice and
Freedom into the world.

I am within you now.
I see Myself, That which I am, within the lotus
of your hearts, arrayed in the colours of your
aspiration, and from this do I derive great joy.
It is that Light within you which has brought Me
to you.
Let it manifest abroad in all its power and glory
and light a pathway for Me in the world.

My Task is to bring you, My friends, before the
Father, before the Gilded Throne of the Shining
One, there to present you to Him and establish
you within Our ranks.

My prophecy holds: I shall take before the Father
all who are ready in this coming time. That is
the Task given to Me by Him Whom we together
serve.

My aim is to present Myself to the world in such
a fashion that no-one will mistake Me for other
than I am.
May you be alert and awake, see Me quickly,
draw yourself and others around Me, and let Me
work through you.

My dear ones, I have need of all those who are
ready for sacrifice, the simple giving of
themselves in love for their brothers.
Do this for Me and for them and restore in the
world the Ways of God.
My Blessing goes with you all.

May the Divine Light and Love and Power of the
One Most Holy God be now manifest within your
hearts and minds.
May this manifestation lead you to express
That which I am.

Message No. 63

February 28th 1979

My dear friends, I am happy indeed to be among
you once more in this way.

My friends and brothers, I am happy, also, to
tell you that My Emergence into full and public
vision has commenced.
For yourselves, soon, therefore, will you see
that the Prince of Peace has returned;
that your Brother of Old, once again, walks
among men;
that the Preacher has returned in a new guise,
but is essentially the Representative of God.

When you see Me you will know, My friends,
that the New Time indeed has begun:
the time of building the New Signposts to the
future;
the time to establish among all peoples correct
relationship and trust;
to advance together in harmony and sharing,
lighting a path for those who will follow.

When you see Me you will know this.
You will know, also, that I come, not as a God
omnipotent to rule, but simply, as an Elder
Brother, to show you the Way.
When you have grasped My intention, you will
see that that Way leads directly to God, for
it is the Way planned for you from the
Beginning.
No man, throughout the history of the world,
has come to his Source by another route.

My friends, brothers and children, know this to
be true and follow Me.
Follow My footsteps into the Light of the future
which today beckons all men.
Let Me lead you therein, and, clasped together
in Love, make salutations to the Father of All.
With His help this will be so.

My intention is to show Myself more openly so
soon now that little time indeed remains to
inform your brothers of My Presence.
Go to, with a will, My friends, make known your
belief in My Return among you and light within
the hearts of all the Light of Truth.

May the Divine Light and Love and Power of the
One Most Holy God be now manifest within your
hearts and minds.
May this manifestation lead you to be ever
imbued with the Truth of the Spirit of God.

Message No. 64

March 6th 1979

My dear friends, I am happy to be among you once
more.

My Emergence proceeds. My Face is known to a
growing body of men in the Centre of My choice,
and soon many of you, for yourselves, will
know that I am here.

My Message tonight is this: prepare all those
who know not yet that I have returned, for My
Presence among them.
Release in them the hope which My return creates
and do for Me and them a service untold.
My need is great for those who see the promise
and the dangers of the time.
I trust you, My brothers and sisters, to work
for Me in this way,
to lift from the world the peril of war,
to relieve the hunger of many,
and to restore well-being to the world.

My Teaching, simple though it is, will show you
the necessity for sharing,
for the creation of a pool of resources from
which all men may take,
the subsitution for greed of co-operation and
trust,
the manifestation of the inner divinity of men.
This manifestation, My friends, must proceed,
for without it the future for man would be
black indeed.

A crisis of decision awaits mankind.
My Love creates a polarity of viewpoints; that
is the Sword which I wield.
My friends, know well where you stand and receive
My Light.
Take care where you place your feet: on the steps
which lead to tomorrow or - oblivion.
Men and women of the world, My brothers, My
children, I appeal to you:
take the upward path into the Light of the Truth
which I bring,
and be enabled to manifest the Gods which you are.
Many there are now who know this to be the only
path for man.
Make it known where you, My friends, stand at
this time.

My Blessings go with you all.

May the Divine Light and Love and Power of the
Everlasting God be now manifest within your
hearts and minds.
May this manifestation lead you into the
expression of your true nature as luminous Gods.

Message No. 65

March 13th 1979

My dear friends, I am happy indeed to be with
you once more, to tell you something of My
Plans and of how these will affect you in this
coming time.

My Plan is to emerge quickly, and, maintaining
a certain rhythm, make known My Presence to
the world.
In My Centre, steps have already been taken
which have allowed many of your brothers and
sisters to see My Face, hear My Words, respond
to My Presence and call to action.
Great, indeed, has been the enthusiasm of your
brothers, which bodes well for the future of
My Mission.
When you, yourselves, see Me, you will, I feel
sure, respond likewise, for within you all does
sit the same Light of Truth, of Justice and
Freedom which I awaken in all who hear Me.
Therefore, My friends, have no fear that mankind
will reject Me.
My Plans are safe in your hands.

My Coming will transform this world, but the
major work of restoration must be done by you.
I am the Architect, only, of the Plan.
You, My friends and brothers, are the willing
builders of the Shining Temple of Truth.
I shall give you the Key of that Temple, and
entering therein shall you know God.

My Masters await, also, your response to Their
guidance.
Give Them your trust and let Them lead you
into the New Dawn,
sharing together the earth's produce,
knowing together the joy of Brotherhood,
manifesting together the divinity within you
all.

The time is short indeed till you shall see Me.
Make best use of this little time to prepare
My Way, to teach all those whom you meet with
the words of Truth which I send to you.
Lead them, too, into the Path of Light and
the Promise which My Return brings to the world.
My Emergence in full vision is imminent. Watch
and wait and sleep not.

May the Divine Light and Love and Power of the
One Most Holy God be now manifest within your
hearts and minds.
May this manifestation lead you to seek and to
find that Essential Being Whom always you
have been.

Message No. 66

March 20th 1979

My dear friends, I am happy indeed to be with
you once more in this way.

My Mission proceeds; all that I hoped for is
being achieved, and augers well for the future.
My Plan is to present Myself to the people of
the world within so short a time that few indeed
will doubt My Presence.
My Words will teach you the Ways of God, the
way forward into the blessed future which I see
before you.
Into the Light of the highest dreams of man
shall I take you.
The Path of Brotherhood will vouchsafe this for
you.

My Plan is to realise within you that which you
truly are, to show you that you stem from the
Godhead Itself, and to that Divine Source must
return.
My Mission will ease for you that passage, that
long journey back to your rightful heritage.
When we meet as brothers, My friends, you will
find in Me a Teacher and Guide Who knows well
the Way, for long since have I made that
self-same journey, and know by heart the
signposts on the way.

Make sure that you miss Me not.
Look well, My friends, for My Appearance may
surprise you.

As a simple man, indeed, am I now among you,
teaching My friends and brothers on the way,
releasing to them My Gifts of Love, Wisdom and
Joy, gathering them to Me as brothers in work.
You, likewise, My dear friends, can rest in
the knowledge that your work for Me and for
your brothers is welcome indeed.
I need you all, all who will take upon themselves
the burden of service to the world, to create
anew this shining world out of the chaos of the
past.
My Blessings go with you all.

May the Divine Light and Love and Power of the
One Most Holy God be now manifest within your
hearts and minds.
May this manifestation lead you to see yourselves
as My co-workers, brothers in Light.

Message No. 67

April 18th 1979

My dear friends, once again I have the pleasure
of speaking to you in this way.

My pleasure is doubled in that I see among you
so many in whom the Light of Truth shines forth.
Great is the joy which this affords Me.

My friends, My brothers and sisters, all proceeds
to plan.
Today there is in this world the fulfillment of the
Prophecies of Old.
My Presence is a fact.
My Love abounds.
My Creative Will plans your future glory.

The tendency today is to reject that which is
simple, to cling to the complex, the erudite and
vague; but all that pertains to Truth, My friends,
will be found to be simple indeed.
Thus am I a simple man.
When you see Me you will know this, and smilingly
take Me as a brother.

Many there are who fear My Advent.
The guilt of ages sits upon their shoulders and
they trust not.
My friends, through Me shall be created the Era
of Trust, the removal of guilt, the Citadel of
Love.

In awe do men await Me.
My friends, I am not God.
As your Brother, your Friend, your Teacher, do
I come. Forget this not.

My plans unfold. My Way is being cleared.
There are growing around Me now those who
recognise Me as the Spirit of the New Time.
They give Me their trust and allegiance.
I speak for them.
When you see Me, My friends and brothers, you,
too, can join this band of workers, this company
of Light, and make manifest the God within.

The time has come for sight and sound of Truth.
I answer the call.
My Mission will restore to men the vision of
God.
Take your place at My side and let Me show you
that vision.

May the Divine Light and Love and Power of the
One Most Holy God fall now upon the hearts and
minds of all.
Through this manifestation may you come quickly
to My side.

Message No. 68

May 4th 1979

I am with you once more, My dear friends.

Tonight I would like to tell you that My Mission
proceeds as planned.
My heart enfolds all those who await My Coming
and, in trust, expect Me.
My Light, which within them shines, has brought
them to this realisation.
In this way do I make known My Advent.

You, My friends, have a unique opportunity to
serve at this time.
You are in receipt of a message of Hope, a
declaration of Truth, and on your judgement
rests your future.
You may take the path that leads to sterile
inaction - that is your right.
But, My friends, why discard an opportunity to
serve your brothers and Me in a most potent
fashion?
Make known the fact of My Presence among you and
see the light of joy awaken in your brothers'
eyes.
Let them, too, share in this manifestation of
hope and promise for the world and take your
place by My side.

Soon you will see Me.
Soon you will know that the One for Whom the
world has waited has arrived, has returned to
serve, to lead man, if he wills, into a new and
blessed time.

My thanks go to those who already work for My
Cause.
Make yourselves one with those valiant ones and
share in this holy work.
There is no need to fear. My plans unfold and
soon the demonstration of peace shall enfold the
world.
Man's way is clear. Behind mankind today stand
their Brothers of Old, their Guides and Leaders,
their Elder Brothers.
Under Their wise guidance mankind shall know the
Peace of God.

May the Divine Light and Love and Power of the
One Most Holy God be now manifest within your
hearts and minds.
May this manifestation lead you in Light to the
Feet of God.

Message No. 69

May 9th 1979

My dear friends, I am happy indeed to be among
you once more, and to see shining from you the
light of Truth.

The key to My Teaching rests, as you know, on
the principle of sharing.
All that men do and all that man will do depends
on this simple and basic truth:
that from the One we call God flows the
Providence for all men.
Accept this as a fact, My friends, and enter
your divinity.
Within you all sits such a God, and through men,
together, can that God manifest.
This is the way planned for you from the
beginning.
When men see this they will know the Truth of
Brotherhood.

My Mission proceeds and steadily My Face and
Voice become known.
Your brothers accept that a new Teacher is among
them and will show them the path to the future.
Likewise, when you see Me, My brothers and
friends, you will join with Me in a great
manifestation of God's Love and create in the
world a new Truth, a new Light, a new and
shining City of Love.
My Task is to lead you therein and perform for
you the requirements of God.
I guard the Gates through which all pass to Him.

If you would serve Me and serve the world, make
known, My friends, that I am here.
In this way can you build the sure wall of Hope
against which the tide of fear will beat in vain.
My Blessings go with you all.

May the Divine Light and Love and Power of the
One Most Holy God be now manifest within your
hearts and minds.
May this manifestation lead you to see yourselves
as My Disciples and helpers.

Message No. 70

May 17th 1979

Good evening, My dear friends. Once again I am
happy to be among you in this way.

My Plan proceeds carefully and well.
Your brothers grow in number around Me and to
them do I give My Blessing and Teaching.
Likewise, in due course, shall I bestow on you
these gifts.

My aim is to spread abroad My net to the widest
horizon, to draw to Me all those in whom My
Light shines, that through them I may work.
This cast can include you, My friends, for I
need all who share with Me the desire to serve
the world.
Take upon yourselves the task of succour and
share My burden.
Share with Me, My friends, in a great work -
nothing less than the transformation of this
world.

My means, as you know, are simple.
I need no other tools than the heart's love of
man.
This, My friends, bestowed on you by That from
which you come, will bring men to the Source of
Love Itself.
Make it manifest, My brothers, and join our
ranks.

I am the Custodian of the Plan of God.
I am the New Direction.
I am the Way for all men.
I hold the Secrets of Old.
I bestow Bliss.

I create the desire for Truth.
I make all men One.
I come to realise My Truth through men.
I am the Saviour of Old.
I am the Teacher of the New.
I am the Guide for the Future Time.
I am the Law Embodied.
I am Truth Itself.
I am your Friend and Brother.
I am your Self.

Take within you That which I am and make That
manifest in the world.

Take within you That which I bestow and create
the City of Light.

Manifest around you That which I pronounce and
become as Gods.

May the Divine Light and Love and Power of the
One Most Holy God be now manifest within your
hearts and minds.
May this manifestation lead you to be encircled
by the Aura of God.

Message No. 71

June 5th 1979

My dear friends, I am happy indeed to be among
you once more in this way.

My Teaching goes forth.
Your brothers respond and bring joy to My heart.
When you see Me, you, too, will share in this
manifestation of God's Love, for I am but the
Spokesman for the One Who sent Me.

My Teaching will show you that there is nothing
in this world which, if needed, cannot be
achieved by man.
Man is a God and requires only to manifest that
divinity to flourish.
My Presence will assure you that this is so, for
My Brothers, the Masters of Wisdom, and I, shall
show you the wonders of your divine nature.
In this way shall you sense your potential and
grow in Light.

My friends, I am among you in this way to ask
you to help Me, to release to your brothers and
sisters the truth of My Presence, the fact of
My Return.
Let them share in the beauty that this promise
brings, and lead them to Me.

My Task unfolds. My work proceeds, and soon in
full vision shall you see and know Me.
My Task will be to take you into the Light of
your own true nature, and realise for you the
Gods you are.

My Task can be lightened, My Path shortened,
by your work.
Let Me ask you, My friends, to do this for Me,
and show your love for your brothers.
Many are the ways to serve.
Choose that which suits you best and serve,
My friends.
Through this act of service will you know God.

May the Divine Light and Love and Power of the
One Most Holy God be now manifest within your
hearts and minds.
May this manifestation lead you into service
for your brothers.

Message No. 72

June 12th 1979

I am with you once again, My dear friends, and
I am happy to be so.

My Forces are gathering around Me.
My Army strengthens from day to day, and in
planned and full array will it march into the
Light, that New Light which I bring to the world.
Listen well, My friends, and you will hear the
jingle of the harness of My troops.
Listen well, My friends, and respond to the
thunder of their drums.
My Call goes forth. I summon all who would go
with Me.
I am among you, My friends, in such a way to call
you, too, to My side.
Take your places, My brothers, in this Company of
Light, and share the joy of the creation of a
New World.

My Task is simple: to lead you into a battle
for Life.
My Aim is vast: to release to you that Life in
abundance.

Have no fear, My friends, the result of that
battle is known to Me.
My Mission proceeds in such a fashion that
victory now is assured.
Let Me lead you then, My friends, into your
heritage, into your true nature as Sons of God.

My Masters are now returning ahead of schedule;
this will allow Them, too, to share in this
great and final battle for the world.

We are behind you, My Brothers and I.
We know the Way; We send you Our Strength.
Take within you this Armour and show your
valour.

The days are numbered when you will see My Face.
Look for the face of a Friend and Guide.

May the Divine Light and Love and Power of the
One Most Holy God be now manifest within your
hearts and minds.
May this manifestation lead you to your places
in our Ranks.

Message No. 73

June 19th 1979

My dear ones, it is with joy that I take this
further opportunity to speak to you in this
manner.

My joy likewise is enlarged when I see within
you the Spirit of Love manifesting.
This brings to My heart a joy which you cannot
know.
Men think of Myself and My Brothers in isolation.
This, My friends, is far from the truth.
Each tremor of Love felt within your heart is
registered in Mine.
This is the simple truth of our relationship.
Know then, My friends, how great is the joy I
feel when I sense your expectation, your release
from fear, and know your trust.

My Way is being prepared.
Make it your task, My brothers and sisters,
to share this burden.
Create around you the atmosphere of trust and
hope into which I soon may enter.
Believe Me, My friends, this is a great work
indeed.
Much depends on the creation of this pool of
trust, this atmosphere of hope.

When I tell you that My feet have already walked
the pavements of cities, this, My friends, is
the truth.
Men are known to Me in the fullest sense:
I know their hopes and fears.
I know their longings and yearnings.
I know their aspiration for good.
Upon all of this I rely.

Make it your avowed task to aid Me in My
coming work.
May it be that you become channels for My Love.
In this way shall you fulfill your destiny, too.

May the Divine Light and Love and Power of the
One Most Holy God be now manifest within your
hearts and minds.
May this manifestation lead you to see yourselves
as My Agents.

Message No. 74

July 3rd 1979

Good evening, My dear friends.

I have come once more in this way to tell you
that My Mission proceeds as planned.
Naught hinders the progress of this holy work,
and soon, for yourselves, you will see the fruit
of My efforts.
The time has come to begin the process of change,
to transform the life of men in such a way that
the God in man shines forth.
This, My friends, is not difficult of accomplishment for within you all sits such a Divine Being.
My Task will be to evoke from you that Shining
Light, and take you to Its Source.

My Masters work also in Their various centres
and through Them proceeds the Plan.
My work is to organise that Plan in such a way
that the least cleavage results.
Much that is loved must go.
Cling not to the old forms.
Much will depend on man's ability to renounce
these outworn structures, and to create a new
and simpler world.
Remember this. Forget not that I come to change
all things.

My Coming brings peace.
Likewise, My Presence brings cleavage.
My Sword, that Love which I am, will separate all
men, will show the True from the false, will
clear the way for the New Light which I bring.
May it be that you can withstand this change
and accept My Light.

Many times before have I told you that My
Appearance is nigh.
Look then carefully, My friends, and miss
Me not.
My Blessing goes with you all.

May the Divine Light and Love and Power of the
One Most Holy God be now manifest within your
hearts and minds.
May this manifestation allow you quickly to
hearken to My Call.

Message No. 75

July 10th 1979

My dear friends, I am happy indeed to be among
you once more in this fashion.

I bring glad tidings.
With joy, I reveal that a further manifestation
of Myself to the public will shortly take place.
Many more, then, of your brothers and sisters
will avail themselves of this occurrence, and
will see and hear Me.
The time when you yourselves may see Me is
short, therefore, indeed.

When you see Me you will know that your Friend
and Brother of Old is with you once again,
that your former Teacher has returned to reveal
to you a further page in the great book of life.
By My counsel you will be enabled to transform
those institutions which require change.
By My example you will be inspired to reach
upwards to the Source of Life Itself.
By My Love you will be taken within the Temple
of Truth, and will see God.

My friends, My brothers, I am with you at last.
For long have I waited to bring to you the Light
of the future.
My Brothers and I look to this coming time as
an opportunity for service.
We, too, My friends, grow by the manifestation
of this divine attribute.
Naught which stems from God but serves, My
brothers.
Learn and believe that this is so.

Through service to man, man will come to God.
It was ever so.
Make a life of service your vow for the future
time and know the Bliss of the Love of God.

My Purpose unfolds.
My Way clears.
My Words are being heard.
My Love encircles all.

May the Divine Light and Love and Power of the
One Most Holy God be now manifest within your
hearts and minds.
May this manifestation lead you, in service,
to the Feet of God.

Message No. 76

July 17th 1979

My dear friends and disciples, it is with
pleasure that I come among you once more in
this way.

My heart leaps with joy when I see above and
around you the Shining Light of My Truth.
Keep it burnished well, My friends, and together
we shall work.

My Presence is evoking change.
My Law begins to be fulfilled.
My Masters return to the world, and the people
wai,t in expectation of Revelation.
The New Truth which I bring will reveal to you
an aspect of God's nature which I, Myself, am.
Through My Presence, this nature will manifest
through those who are ready, and they, My brothers
and sisters, shall see the Face of God.
Long ago I told you that God is love.
Verily, this is so.
But that Love, My friends, flows from a higher
Source and That I shall reveal to you.

My Plan is to come before the people stage by
stage.
Those who would know Me must look for a simple
man indeed, a Brother and a Friend, a Teacher
and a Guide, a lover of God and men.
When you see Me you will come to know the
nature of God as Light and Love and Will.
May it be that these divine aspects shall
reflect through you.
When this is so I may work through you.

I need you.
I need you all to share with Me in the
reconstruction of this world, to restore to men
their faith and joy, to release the wherewithal
to live to the needy of this earth, and so
restore balance.
My Task is to show you the method;
yours is to act and implement My Plan.
I know I can trust and call on you.
My Love embraces all.

May the Divine Light and Love and Power of the
One Most Holy God be now manifest within your
hearts and minds.
May this manifestation take you quickly, in joy,
to your Source.

Message No. 77

July 26th 1979

My dear friends, I am happy indeed to be with you
once more in this way.

My Emergence takes place in mounting rhythm.
My brothers and sisters, within a few days, shall
see and hear Me.
I shall speak to them of the need for Love and
Justice in the affairs of men, in the affairs of
State, in the association of peoples; and I
shall show them that without this Divine Love
and Justice all men will perish.
My hope is - nay, My brothers, My knowledge is -
that mankind will respond to My Call.
I know this to be so.
I know that within men sits a Divine Being,
Whose Plan it is that Love and Justice should
triumph.
This being so, the end is assured.

But not all see the necessity for change, for
the transformation of this world, for the
implementation of sharing, co-operation and
trust.
When My simple Law, the Law of Love, is obeyed,
all of this will ensue.
Therefore, My friends, I speak simply of Love
and Trust.

Many today know that these aspects count, but
realise not their central place.
My friends, all life depends for its existence
on the Love of God.
This simple Truth I teach.
Make it your own.
Make it central to your lives, and advance
with Me.

My Brothers, the Masters of Wisdom, will show
you the simple path to the future, a future
planned for you by the One we call God.
That path can be followed by all men, and
through My Agency shall they come to God.

We are with you, My Brothers and I.
We send you Hope.
We send you Courage.
We ask for your trust.
We need your allegiance.
We count on your Divinity.

May the Divine Light and Love and Power of the
One Most Holy God be now manifest within your
hearts and minds.
May this manifestation lead you to see
yourselves as My colleagues and workers in
the Light.

Message No. 78

August 2nd 1979

My dear friends, I am happy indeed to be among
you in this way and to tell you that My Plans
unfold.

I have around Me now a group of brothers and
sisters who see Me as their leader and guide to
the future.
To them do I speak of man's troubles, of man's
imperfections, of man's need for change ;
but also I tell them that man is a God,
a Divine Being of Light, Who one day shall
stand arrayed as such.

The choice is man's alone.
If he chooses the path which I shall indicate,
that Divinity shall verily shine forth.
Otherwise, My brothers and sisters, the future
for man would be fateful indeed.

But, My friends, I know beforehand your answer
and choice.
Through your love - the love in your heart for
your brothers - have no fear, My dear ones,
you will choose correctly.
This love will radiate throughout the world
and on this you may count.
My Presence guarantees that this shall be so.
Already, the changes are occurring in such
magnitude that victory is assured.

When you see Me, you will know that your Elder
Brother has taken this step through love of
His brethren.
That, My friends, is why I am now among you.

164

But also you have called Me; your cry for help
has reached My ears, and gladly do I answer
that call.

May the coming time bring to you the knowledge
of My Presence, the sight of My Appearance,
the sound of My Words; and when you see Me and
hear Me, hearken to Me.
I need all those who long to serve,
who wish to fulfill their purpose in life,
who see this life as a step on the way, and
accept the lever of service as the greatest
gift.
Make then your choice: to serve and follow Me,
or relinquish progress.

I am with you always.

May the Divine Light and Love and Power of the
One and Holy God be now manifest within your
hearts and minds.
May this manifestation lead you in Light to My
side.

Message No. 79

August 28th 1979

My dear friends, I am happy indeed to be with
you once more in this fashion, and to tell you
that My work proceeds well.

Already, many of your brothers in My Centre have
heard My words, have seen My face, and have
responded to My Call.
Soon, for yourselves, you will know, and awaken
to, the fact of My Presence.
When you see Me you will know that the time for
action has come, for I count on you, My friends,
to act in implementing My Plan.
For many of you, this is an old and well-known
mode of life; you are servers come to serve
your brothers.
It is as such that I shall call on you, and I
value highly your help.
Without that willing help My Mission would be
a burden indeed.

Now that I am among you, I have discovered even
more keenly that mankind is ready to share.
Within all those who hear Me I see the burning
Light of Justice and Truth.
I voice simply their desire, and thus evoke
that Truth.
So will it be with you, My friends, for even as
I speak I see shining within you this Divine
Light.
Let it shine brightly forth, My dear friends,
and show the way for your brothers.

My coming is not without problems, for I do
engender in all I meet a sense of a new and
mysterious future.
This causes many to fear, but without cause, My
friends.
All should know that the future for all men,
through My Presence, is bright indeed.
A new and wholesome Brotherhood will flourish
among men, and the Justice of God shall be
found arrayed in the Glory of God.
I come to teach you this.
I come to show you the way.
My friends, I count on you.

May the Divine Light and Love and Power of the
One Most Holy God be now manifest within your
hearts and minds.
May this manifestation lead you to see yourselves
as Brothers all.

Message No. 80

September 6th 1979

My dear friends, I am happy indeed to be with you
once more in this fashion, and to tell you that
My work in the world proceeds well.

All that I intend takes place.
All that I attempt succeeds.
When I make Myself known you will know that the
moment to inaugurate God's Plan has come.
This Plan, My dear friends, contains within it
the future for all men and all things in the
world. With the help of man himself, that Plan
will work out.
My Presence among you guarantees that this is so.

I embody the Plan of God.
I am the Benefactor.
I reach men through Love.
I teach men through Law.
I send Blessings to the world.
I engender Hope.
The City of Love will be built through Me.

The Masters of Wisdom, My Disciples, are
Themselves among you; slowly They take Their
places in Their Centres.
When My Name is known, Their Names, likewise,
shall be known.

My brothers and sisters, take within you that
which I am, and prepare to see a new Light.
Hold within you that which I give, and know the
meaning of Truth.
Release within you that which you eternally are,
and become Gods.

I am among you now.
I see your dreams of Trust and Love.
I feel your aspiration and hope.
I shall take these to My Heart and accomplish
them for you.

I am your Mentor.
I am your highest wish.
I am your clearest light.
I am your heart's love.

I shall take you to that Blessed Country which
I call Love.
I shall show you God dwelling therein, and
evoke from you that Divinity.

Hold fast to your Truth.
Hold fast to your Light.
Hold fast, My friends, My brothers, to your Love.
Manifest that Love and follow Me.

May the Divine Light and Love and Power of the
One Most Holy God be now manifest within your
hearts and minds.
May this manifestation lead you to see yourselves
as each other.

Message No. 81

September 12th 1979

My dear friends, I am happy indeed to be with
you once more, and to magnetize your aspiration
in this way.

My Coming evokes in man a desire for change, a
desire for betterment, however expressed.
My energies engender in man divine discontent.
All that is useless in our structures must go.
There are many such which are unworthy of man
today.

Man is an emerging God and thus requires the
formation of modes of living which will allow
this God to flourish.
How can you be content with the modes within
which you now live: when millions starve and
die in squalor; when the rich parade their
wealth before the poor; when each man is his
neighbour's enemy; when no man trusts his
brother?
For how long must you live thus, My friends?
For how long can you support this degradation?

My Plan and My duty is to reveal to you a new
way, a way forward which will permit the divine
in man to shine forth.
Thus do I speak gravely, My friends and brothers.
Hearken well to My words.
Man must change or die; there is no other course.
When you see this you will gladly take up My
Cause, and show that for man exists a future
bathed in Light.

My Teaching is simple:
Justice, Sharing and Love are Divine Aspects.
To manifest his divinity man must embrace these
three.

May the Divine Light and Love and Power of the
One Most Holy God be now manifest within your
hearts and minds.
May this manifestation bring you to the
realisation of your part in the Great Plan.

Message No. 82

September 18th 1979

My dear friends, I am happy indeed to be among
you once more in this fashion, and to set before
you some guidelines for the future.

My task will be to show you how to live together
peacefully as brothers.
This is simpler than you imagine, My friends,
for it requires only the acceptance of Sharing.
Sharing, indeed, is divine.
It underlies all progress for man.
By its means, My brothers and sisters, you can
come into correct relationship with God; and
this, My friends, underlies your lives.
When you share, you recognise God in your
brother.
This is a Truth, simple, but until now difficult
for man to grasp.
The time has come to evidence this Truth.

By My Presence the Law of Sharing will become
manifest.
By My Presence man will grow to God.
By the Presence of Myself and My Brothers,
the New Country of Love shall be known.
Take, My friends, this simple Law to your hearts.
Manifest Love through Sharing, and change the
world.
Create around you the atmosphere of Peace and
Joy, and with Me make all things new.

My Coming portends change.
Likewise, grief at the loss of the old
structures.
But, My friends, the old bottles must be broken —
the new wine deserves better.

My friends, My brothers, I am near you now.
I see above and around you your aspiration for
Love and Joy.
I know this to be widespread in mankind; this
makes possible My return.

Let Me unveil for you your divine inheritance.
Let Me show you the wonders of God which yet
await you.
Allow Me to take you simply by the hand and
lead you to the Forest of Love,
the Glade of Peace,
the River of Truth.

Take My hand, My friends, and know this to be
yours, now.

May the Divine Light and Love and Power of the
One Most Holy God be now manifest within your
hearts and minds.
May this manifestation lead you in trust to the
Country I call Love.

Message No. 83

September 28th 1979

My dear friends and disciples, I am happy
indeed to be among you once more in this way.

My Plans unfold.
My brothers and sisters are awakening to My
Presence and for themselves chart a new course.
This is encouraging indeed, for, despite My
Plans, mankind's will is free.
When, therefore, I witness man's response,
great is My joy.

My Teaching is simple, as you know:
Love, Justice and correct sharing are necessary
for man to live.
Those around Me now, in My Centre, are learning
this, are responding to My Call and awakening
to the promise of the future.
For you too shall this be so, for within you
now I see the same divine intention.
Therefore, My friends, fear not for My Mission.

My Plan is to come before the world so soon
that only the most abject mind will deny My
Presence.
Great, even now, are the changes which occur:
The nations grow together in a new bond of
harmony. Witness for yourselves these events.
When My Face is seen on a wider scale, this
transformation will gain a new impetus, and
much, quickly, will be achieved.

I trust you, My friends, to help Me in this
work, to take your part in this Plan of God;
for My Father has sent Me to show you the way
to Him.
That Task do I lightly take up.

May the Divine Light and Love and Power of the
One Most Holy God be now manifest within your
hearts and minds.
May this manifestation prove to you the fact
of My Advent.

Message No. 84

My dear friends, once again I am with you and
am happy to be so close to you.

Many of My friends and disciples in the world
know now that My Presence is an established fact,
but many more by far are still ignorant of this
blessed truth.
Therefore, My friends, My brothers, My disciples,
it behoves you to work harder and thus make
known on the widest scale that I am among you.
In doing this you serve your brothers in a way
second to none; at this time, nothing finer in
service can be achieved by you.
Therefore, My friends, the divinity within you,
shining as always, exhorts you to this measure
to aid My Cause.

Learn the Ways of God, My brothers, by following
My Precepts.
My Teaching, simple as it is, will show you the
straight path to the Source, and along that
Shining Path are those Sentinels and Guardians
Who know the Way.
We, My Brothers and I, will show you that Way
and, trusting, you will see God.
My Way, the Way of Truth, of Light, of simple
Brotherhood, is the Way for all men.
Each one among you can take this open path to
God, and under My Guidance come to know God.

Where, My friends, are the alternatives?
There is nowhere else to go.
All around you God shines in Its Glory;
within you and around you shines this Blessed
Truth.
The day is coming, My friends, when men
everywhere shall see this Truth and stand
ablaze with the Glory of the Divine Source.

Look not then for other ways to go, for the path
is clear, the steps of ascent are hewn, the
signposts are set, the Guides are at hand;
the end is Divinity Itself.
Who, My friends, knowing this could accept less?

My Plans further unfold.
My Face and Words are seen and heard.
My Emergence proceeds apace, and soon the world
will know that their Teacher has come.
Make it your task, then, to make known these
facts, this Promise, and inherit your glory.

May the Divine Light and Love and Power of the
One Most Holy God be now manifest within your
hearts and minds.
May this manifestation lead you quickly to see
and accept your service.

Message No. 85

October 12th 1979

My friends, My dear ones, I am happy to be among you once more in this way.

My Plans progress. My face and voice are known to many of your brothers and gradually My Presence becomes known.
Taking stock of My Mission thus far, I see changes so radical that My Plans unfold sooner than I anticipated.
This being so, My brothers, My face will become known to you before long.

When you see Me, My friends, know then that the hand of your Friend is yours to grasp;
the Love of your Brother is yours to absorb;
the Teaching of That One is yours to hear.
Know this, My friends, and take responsibility for reaching your brothers with these truths.

My Plan is that the world should be changed by man.
The Law forbids all else.
Therefore, My friends, I depend on you to execute My Plan, and thus prepare the New World.

My Teaching will show you that the Law of God holds for all men.
Naught can stand outside this Law.
When men see this they will gladly accept the simple Law of Love, and make it manifest.

Wherever I look today around the world, I see
the shining points of Light of My people, those
on whom I rely.
These beacons of Light shall bring all men to
Me, and thus the Plan will unfold.
May it be that you will gather yourselves around
Me in this way, that My Light may kindle your
flame; and so together we can transform this
world.

The Path is not easy, My friends; much there is
to do.
But through simple Love and Brotherhood all
shall be achieved.

Make no mistake, My friends, Maitreya needs
you - needs you to further the Plan which He
brings, which is the Plan of God.
I trust you, My friends, not to forsake Me.

**May the Divine Light and Love and Power of the
One Most Holy God be now gathered around you all.**

Message No. 86

October 17th 1979

My dear friends, I am happy indeed to be among
you once again.

My friends, My dear ones, My comrades of old,
many times before have I exhorted you to work
to prepare My Way.
Once again may I say how vital this work is.
The more who know that I have returned the
sooner My Face shall be known.
Let My Message speak to all men.
Let My Words go forth.
Send them to your brothers near and far and
awaken them, too, to My Advent.

My public work proceeds.
I plan from day to day and watch carefully man's
response.
In this way the rhythm of My Emergence is set,
and so you see, My friends, how your work
influences My Plan.

My Masters will show you that there is little
which you cannot effect if you but try.
All is possible to man.
All that man needs is provided by his Source.
The Great Provider remembers His children.
Look not then askance at the future time but
welcome it with open arms and joy, knowing that
brotherhood and trust will be the norm.

My friends, My brothers and sisters, take stock
of where you now stand:
Are you ready to go with Me to the Blessed Isle
of Love?
Are you ready to share with all that which you
now have?
Are you prepared, My friends, to look Life
bravely in the eye and see it as a challenge to
achievement?
Naught can hold you back if you go with Me.
Nothing will remain of the old inertia, but
clasped in Light and Love, you, My friends, can
know the joy of nearness to the Father; that joy
which it is My privilege to bestow on you.
Take then, My friends, your courage in your
hands and follow Me back to your Source.
Naught can go wrong, My friends, Maitreya is
with you!

May the Divine Light and Love and Power of the
Everlasting God be now manifest within your
hearts and minds.
May this manifestation bring you to the
achievement of your own soul's purpose.

Message No. 87

November 16th 1979

My dear friends, I am happy to be among you once
more in this fashion.

My Mission proceeds well, even beyond My
expectations.
For this reason alone you may see Me soon.
My Plan is to emerge as quickly as may be, and
to evoke from you that service which, My friends,
I know burns within your hearts.

For many reasons am I here.
Many are the claims upon My Love, My Will, but,
above all, to show you once again that man's
purpose is to serve both God and man am I here.
When you see this, you will enter a field of
endeavour which awaits all those who would go
with Me.
Trust Me, My friends; trust that as your Elder
Brother I know the Way, for that Way, My friends,
has been trodden by all Those Whom you call
Master.
The Way to God, My brothers, is through service
and love.
That simple path shall I place before you and
invite you to tread.

My dear friends, look around you at the
happenings in the world and ask yourselves:
"Is this not strange? How come we by this new
Light?"
If you are true to the light within you, you
will see that My Presence evokes this change.
Thus will you know that I am here.

Thus can you share the burden of preparation
for My Emergence and thus can you know the joy
of service.
Take upon yourselves, My brothers, a part of
this burden; make it your own; dedicate
yourselves to making My Presence known to your
brothers far and near.
In this way can you serve Me and them.

My Teachings go forth.
Many are those now, in My Centre, who listen
and act, filled with joy that a new Light is
here, a new Promise beckons, a New World is in
the making.
Share soon then, My friends, in this aspiration
and Truth, and release the God Who within you
dwells.

Take to your hearts, My friends, this message
of Hope; spread it abroad among your brothers
and tell them that Maitreya has come, that the
Lord of Love is here.
Tell them this, My friends, and know the bliss
of serving the Truth.

May the Divine Light and Love and Power of the
One Most Holy God enter now your hearts and
minds and bring you to the realization of your
Divinity.

Message No. 88

November 20th 1979

My friends, I am happy indeed to be among you
once more in this way.

I come to tell you that My Plan proceeds
smoothly and well.
All proceeds to plan; all My hopes are being
fulfilled, and the Day of Declaration draws near.

Soon will you see Me in full vision and, as you
do, realise that for many this meeting is not
the first.
Many of you have served Me before, long, long ago,
and coming now into the world stand ready once
again.
Know this, My friends, and seize the opportunity
now offered to serve Me and the world.
Know this, My brothers, and take part in this
Plan of God for your fulfilment.
Many are the ways to serve; many are the paths
of ascent. No-one today need feel deprived of
a mode of service, of a path forward to the
future.
All paths, all means, flow to God.
Take, My friends, the nearest of these paths
and with Me serve your brothers.

When you see Me, you will see a friend, a
helper, not a God.
Know this, My brothers, and work with Me as
equals.
Let fear not cloud the bond between us, but let
us together, as friends and brothers, serve the
Plan.

The means are simple as you know.
The way forward is steep but climbable.
The Path of Ascent is signposted.
My Masters will guide you on each turn of that
Path, and show you the next step.

Hold out your hands to Me, My friends, and let
Me lift you into the Light.
Raise your heads to that Light, My brothers, and
let Me show you the Face of God.
Kneel with Me before His Divine Feet and know
the joy of communion with Truth.

Let Me show you, My friends, that you are Sons
of God.
Let Me take you, My brothers, on the Way to God.
Let Me show you, My dear ones, the Image and
wonders of God.

Come with Me and know the New Truth.

May the Divine Light and Love and Power of the
One Most Holy God be now manifest within your
hearts and minds.
May this manifestation bring you to His Blessed
Feet.

Message No. 89

November 28th 1979

My dear friends, I am happy to be with you once
again in this fashion.

My brothers, you have heard something of My
Plans, of My Teachings, and know to look soon
for My Face.
Thus it is, My friends.
Thus do I speak to your brothers.
Thus do I make known the needs of the time.
Thus will be established in men correct
relationship to man and God.
My Mission is to unfold for you the Divine
Plan, to administer the Will and Purpose of
God, and to return you to your Source.

My Masters, too, stand ready to serve.
Their ranks will be filled by you, men and
women of the world, and so release Them for
the Higher Way.

At the foot of the mountain, My brothers, the
climb upward seems steep indeed, but when the
first steps have been taken the progress is
rapid, and near the mountain top winged feet
shall you have, and from that height shall you
see the glories of God.
Thus shall it be, My friends and brothers.
I, Maitreya, promise.

Take Me to your hearts as I have taken you to
Mine.
Work with Me, My friends, and know Me as a
Guide.
Help Me to re-instate in the world the Plan of
God, the destined Will of our Divine Source.
Help Me to do this, My friends, and inherit
your greatness.

My Steps resound.
My Law unfolds.
My words find response in the hearts of many.
The time is not far off when the New World
will be seen,
the Country of Love approached,
the City of Truth built.
Take My hands, My friends, and let us together
build.

May the Divine Light and Love and Power of the
One Most Holy God be now manifest within your
hearts and minds.
May this manifestation lead you to respond to
My Presence among you.

Message No. 90

December 6th 1979

My dear friends, I am happy indeed to be so close
to you once again, and to release to you some
further fragments of My Plan.

My work proceeds.
My Law finds response in the hearts of men.
My Love permeates these hearts and awakens in
them a new Light.
Thus do I bring to men the knowledge of My
Presence.
Thus do I establish in their midst a reservoir
of Truth.
Thus do I bring men to the readiness for a
Divine Gift.

My purpose tonight is to tell you that My face
is seen and known by so many of your brothers
that now My Message bears fruit.
They respond to Me as you, My friends, will do
when you see Me; when My Love surrounds you as
It now surrounds them; as My simple Truth raises
the Light in you, and you embrace that Truth.

I am the Messenger of God's Truth.
I am the Perfect One.
I am the Means to the Light.
I make smooth the Path for all men.
I condition God's Truth.
I wield the sword.
I embody God's Plan.
I am the Exponent of Love.
I am the Manipulator of Will.
I am the Revealer of Truth.

Take that which I am within your hearts and
reveal the God you are.

I shall place before you all the purpose of God.
I shall lead before the Throne of God all who
are ready.
I shall kneel with you at His Divine Feet and
together shall we salute His Grace.

I am the Intention of God.
I am the Revealer of God's Law.
I am the Truth Embodied.
I am Cause and Knowledge of Cause.
I am Love Itself.
I come before you as a simple man.
I come as a Brother and Friend.
I shall return you to your Source.
I am among you till the end of the Age.

My Love surrounds you always.
My Heart beats in rhythm with yours.
My Hand shall guide you and protect you.
My Love has no bounds.
Know Me as your Friend and Counsellor.
See God through Me.

Take that which I am within your hearts and
become the Gods you are.
Take within you that which I give and reveal
the Light.
Accept My Gift and know the Source.

May the Divine Light and Love and Power of the
One Most Holy God be now manifest within your
hearts and minds.
May this manifestation lead you to serve in the
accomplishment of My Mission.

My dear friends, I am happy indeed to be with
you once more in this fashion.

My friends, I am emerging so quickly now that
little time will elapse until you see My Face.
When you see Me you will know that your Brother
of Old, Maitreya Himself, is among you.
I shall call on you to work for Me and for the
Plan.
I know, My friends, that I may count on you.

My Teaching is this:
Learn to share, to grasp your brother's hand
and know him as yourself.
Teach this simple Truth and you teach the Law of
God.

My Presence creates an atmosphere of new trust,
of new possibilities for mutual understanding.
Seize, then, these God-given opportunities to
grow in service.

My Masters are Themselves returning to the
world; one by one They take up Their stations
among you.
Soon Their Presence will more potently be felt,
and in this way shall They establish the New
Vanguard, those whose task it is to build the
structures of the coming time.
May you know Them before long.
May you give Them your trust and work with Them
for your brothers.

Know Me as one of yourselves, as a simple man
indeed, come among you to serve you and guide
you, to teach you and love you, to show you the
Path to God.

Many are gathering around Me now.
My Army grows.
My Light embraces all.
My Love fills their hearts.
My Will upholds them.
My Shield covers them.
My Truth inspires them.

You, too, My friends, can find the path to My
ranks.
Take it quickly, My brothers, and advance with
Me.

May the Divine Light and Love and Power of the
One Most Holy God be now manifest within your
hearts and minds.
May this manifestation lead you to find Me
quickly,
and to serve at My side.

Message No. 92

December 19th 1979

My dear friends and disciples, I am happy indeed
to be with you once again in this fashion.

My need for disciples who realise the danger of
the time is great.
I need, also, those who sense My Presence to
make known this Promise to their brothers.
All who share the hope that mankind should live
in peace together work for Me.
Peace, Sharing and Justice are central to My
Teaching.
Wherever the Light of these Truths shines I turn
My eye, and through the channel of that Light
do I send My Love.
Thus do I work.
Thus through you do I change the world.

My friends, I need you in other ways:
I need your capacity for Joy, to awaken this
Divine Aspect in the hearts of all men, to show
them that ahead of mankind stretches the luminous
Path of Truth, the direct Path to the Source.
Manifested Love and Joy will take you quickest
there.

My friends, My brothers and sisters, I need you
too to act for Me, to state aloud My Intentions,
My requirements as the Representative of God: to
show men that the world is One; that men are
brothers; that the Law of Love and Justice must
be implemented if mankind would survive.
Tell your brothers this, My friends, and prepare
them for Me.

Awaken in their hearts the readiness to share,
and light their lamp.
Create an atmosphere of Love and Joy and pave
smooth My Way.
Manifest the Love which I send you, demonstrate
the Gods which you are, and usher in a new and
better time.
Do this for Me, My friends and brothers, and
rejoice soon in My Appearance among you.

My Emergence proceeds.
My Plans unfold.
My Message at this time of joyous celebration
is this:
Awaken anew the Love in the hearts of your
brothers and teach them to share.

My Plan is that you shall see Me soon.
When you do you will see your Friend and Brother
of Old, the Advocate of Love, the Administrator
of Will, the Creator through you of the New and
Blessed Time.

May the Divine Light and Love and Power of the
One Most Holy God be now manifest within your
hearts and minds.
May this manifestation lead you to realise your
true usefulness to Me and to the Plan.

My dear friends, I am happy indeed to be so close
to you once again.

My Mission continues with success.
My Heart enfolds all who think of Me.
My Love embraces all who love their brothers.
Know this to be true and call on My Aid.

When you see Me you will know that there is among
you now a simple man of God, a man like other men,
but One Who from time long past has followed a
certain Path, Who knows well that Path and can
lead you thereon.
That Path to God, My friends, is the Treasure I
hold for you.
Awaken your minds and hearts to this possibility
and reach the Goal.
The way is simple, the way is sure.
My Teaching will guide you there.

No man need fear for the future when My Shield
shall cover him.
No man need fear want when My Principle governs.
No man need feel separate from God when My Way
beckons.

Hold yourselves in readiness for My words.
Take your places at My side.
Make manifest the God within and transform the
world.

My heart aches when I see so many needlessly die;
hunger and pestilence stalk the earth.
Nothing so moves Me to grief as this shame.
The crime of separation must be driven from this
world.
I affirm that as My Purpose.

I address you tonight as those who seek the
Truth.
My friends, the Truth stands among you.
The Truth is in your hearts.
The Truth, My friends, My brothers and sisters,
is Love and Sharing, Justice and Freedom.
Make these manifest in your lives and
communities and re-establish the Plan of God.

My voice will soon be heard, My Teaching known,
My Love felt.
May it be that you will quickly see Me, come
towards Me, gather around Me, work with Me,
Know Me and love Me, know God and love God
through Me.

May the Divine Love and Light and Power of the
One Most Holy God be now manifest within your
hearts and minds.
May this manifestation reveal to you your true
worth as Children of God.

Message No. 94

January 31st 1980

My dear friends, once again I am with you and
am happy to be so.

My Plans unfold.
My Mission prospers.
My Way is being cleared.
Many now in the world know of My Presence and
help in all ways.
Still more is needed from you who believe, My
friends.
If in a final major effort you can inform the
world that I am here, My Face will shortly be
seen by all.
I trust you, My brothers and sisters, to work
thus for Me.

When you see Me, you will understand the reasons
for your presence in the world.
You are here, My friends, to serve the Plan of
God.
You are here, each of you, from love of your
brothers.
You are here, too, to learn, to expand your
knowledge of that Plan and to progress along
the Path.
That is the truth of your existence at this
time.
Take heed, then, of this opportunity which I
present to you: to share with Me in My work of
succour, to ease My Burden, to unfold the God
within you and to lead your brothers to the
Light.

Many there are whom I call.
Many there are who wait and listen.
Few there are, indeed, who seize the time and
act.

196

These few are My people.
May you become one of them.

Let Me say this, My friends:
Without your willing help naught may be done.
I come to lead and teach, not to enforce.
Take, then, to your hearts this, My appeal,
and work with Me, for Me, for your brothers,
and so save the world.

Many hear Me now and give Me their trust, attune
their thoughts to Me and follow My lead.
Soon will emerge a body of prepared men who know
the needs of the time, who live to serve, who
love their brothers.
Make yourselves one with them and follow Me.
I shall lead you not astray.

May the Divine Light and Love and Power of the
One Most Holy God be now manifest within your
hearts and minds.
May this manifestation lead you in Light to the
feet of God.

Message No. 95

February 14th 1980

My dear friends, I am happy to be among you
once more in this way, and to tell you that
My first phase of emergence is almost over.

Within weeks many more of your brothers shall
see Me.
Within months a large section of the world will
know that I am here.
Whether they recognize Me or not, My Face will
be seen.

I tell you this My friends:
Look hard and listen well, for My voice is being
heard, My words are turning the hearts of men to
the Truth.
My Love pervades the hearts of all those who
seek that Truth, who long for its establishment
and thus prepare My Way.

First of all you will see a simple man, one of
yourselves.
Know Him as a man Who has travelled for long on
the Path to God, Who seeks to take you with Him
on that Sacred Way and lead you to His Divine
Feet.

Take My simple words to your hearts.
There let them blossom and flower and bring
forth the Light.
Take, too, to your hearts My Love.
Send this to your brothers and make Light the
dark.
Hold fast to My Purpose which is to take man to
God.
Help Me thus, My friends, and serve well the
Plan.

My Teachings are simple, My words likewise.
All that I say is quickly understood.
There is nothing difficult about the Truth
of God.
The Truth of God, My friends, resides in the
hearts of all men.
That simplicity is yours to unfold.
I, your Guide, shall show you the way.

The time has come to show My Face on a wider
scale.
In this way men will know that the Son of Man
is among them once more.

The Love of God manifests through Me, the Bliss
of that Love is yours to take.
Stretch forth your hands, My friends and
brothers, and sup well, drink deeply of the
Blessing of God.

May the Divine Light and Love and Power of the
One Most Holy God be now manifest within your
hearts and minds.
May this manifestation lead you to see quickly
the Light, the Love and the Truth which I bring.

February 19th 1980

My dear friends, My dear ones, I am happy indeed
to be among you once more in this fashion.

My task begins.
As I emerge I shall place before the world the
necessity for change.
These changes, My friends, are God-given.
Man requires, as he moves towards God, to
demonstrate that divinity.
All man's structures must shine with the Divine
Light.
All man's ways of thought must reveal the God
within.
This truth, My friends, is at the basis of change.
When you see this you will gladly accept this
need.

My friends, I am with you tonight in a special
way, in a new form, closer than ever before, to
awaken in you the light of the Truth which I
bring.
That Truth, My friends, is Brotherhood and
Sharing, Justice and Love.
Where these aspects are present you will know Me.

Take heart from all I say, My brothers, for the
way ahead for man shines brightly indeed.
Naught there is to fear, My friends, for all
will be well.
My Mission prospers, and My Presence guarantees
this future.

I am here tonight to tell you that soon for
yourselves you shall see and hear Me.
Make this time shorter, if you will, and make
known My Presence.
When you see Me you will see your Friend and
Brother, One Who for long has waited for this
time, to clasp again the hands of His brothers
and to share their life.

My friends, My Presence is established, My Love
flows to you, My Joy will be yours, My Truth
shared, My Father known.
With your help all will be achieved.

My Task is to show you the way to God, to
outline that simple path, to take your hand and
lead you to His Divine Feet, and so complete
His Plan.
My Masters are with you also. In gathering
numbers They shall be among you.
When you see Us you will know that
the time of God has come,
the Age of Reason and Love begun,
the meaning of life restored,
the Principle of Love demonstrated,
the Will of God fulfilled.

May the Divine Light and Love and Power of the
One Most Holy God be now manifest within your
hearts and minds.
May this manifestation lead you in trust to
My side.

Message No. 97

February 28th 1980

My beloved friends, I am happy indeed to be so
close to you once again.

My Plan is to reveal My Presence shortly on a
much wider scale and to show men that the New
Age is dawning, that the recipe for change is
Sharing and Brotherhood, Justice and Love.
To My Banner I shall call those who would walk
with Me.

Join My Army, My friends and brothers, and
cleanse this world of hate.
Sharpen the Sword of Love, My brothers, close
your ranks around Me, and valiantly together
into the future let us march.

My Principles take hold of men's minds.
My Love penetrates their hearts
My simple words find response, and My Law
begins to govern.
Thus may you say with Me, My friends, that the
future for Man is bright, that the Love of God
is established abroad, and the Law shall
flourish.

Many there are who doubt My Presence.
Many there are who seek for Me in vain, looking
upwards to the sky and, finding Me not, cast Me
out from their hearts.
The simple Truth, My brothers, is that I am a
man among men, living among you as such, knowing
and feeling your griefs and needs, loving and
caring for you, desiring to share with you the
Blessings of God.

Look upon Me thus, My friends and brothers, and
know the meaning of trust, know the value of
Love, know the Blessings of God's Plan for all
men.

May you be ready when I appear before you.
May you be ready for the changes which must
ensue.
May you gladly, eagerly, accept these changes
and make new this world.
Naught stands still on Earth, My friends; all
must change and die.
The dead remnants of the past must likewise find
themselves as ashes.
From these ashes shall arise the Temple of God,
the City of Love.
May you know this to be true.
I am with you always.

May the Divine Light and Love and Power of the
One Most Holy God be now manifest within your
hearts and minds.
May this manifestation lead you to be ever
mindful of your true nature as Gods.

Message No. 98

March 5th 1980

My dear friends and disciples, I am with you
once more.

My heart embraces you all.
My Love enfolds you.
My Law will guide you.
My Teaching will show you the Path to the Source.
Hold steadfast to the truth of your Being and
follow Me.

My Way is a simple way indeed.
Naught hinders on the Path to God through Love.
This I shall teach.
This shall I demonstrate, and when you see how
simple is this Way, My Plans shall become yours.

My Masters are gathering in strength.
My forces expand.
My simple means attract the good in man.
When you see Me you will know that the time has
come to serve, to lift yourselves and your
brothers through service to the world.
This Way, My Way, will take you quickly to God.
My Masters, too, know this Path and under Their
instruction shall you realize your Godhead.

My purpose is to show man that he need fear no
more, that all of Light and Truth rests within
his heart, that when this simple fact is known
man will become God.

God's nature is to love.
God's purpose is to serve.
God is known through Sharing and Justice.
Spread abroad these simple Truths, My friends,
and perform a mighty act.

My Presence will soon be known to all.
My face will soon be seen by many.
My words shall touch the hearts of all those
who love their brothers and thus work with Me.
Make it your resolve, My friends, to work thus
for the world and speed the inauguration of the
Age of Beauty, Reason and Love.

May the Divine Light and Love and Power of the
One Most Holy God be now manifest within your
hearts and minds.
May this manifestation take you swiftly to the
Heart of the Great Father.

Message No. 99

March 11th 1980

My dear friends, I am happy to be with you once more.

My methods produce results.
From My point of vision great changes can be seen.
Therefore, My friends, I have decided to emerge into full and public work more quickly than planned.
So, My friends, you shall the sooner see Me.

May I ask you, My brothers and sisters, to act as My agents, to tell your friends and those you meet that Maitreya is here, that the Son of Man walks abroad once more, that the Teacher for the New Age is among you, and that that Age has begun.
Speak thus, My friends and brothers, and know the joy of service.
Speak thus, My dear ones, and light a lamp for Me.

When you see Me you will know that you have not worked in vain, that your Brother of Old is with you, that your Friend and Guide is among you, that your Teacher of Old has returned to show you the simple Path to God.
Wherefore, then, My friends, your fear?
Make it your task to do this for Me and take within your hands the reins of progress.

My Plans are laid.
My Masters silently enter Their centres. One by one They take Their places among you.
My joy is unbounded as I watch the response of mankind.
My simple Truth, that God and Love are One, is awakening man to the promise of the future.
This makes simple My Task.

My friends, show yourselves as men and women
ready to act as heroes, as warriors of old,
filled with joy and love, ready for the tasks
of succour and love which will fall to you.
Have no fear, My brothers, your shoulders shall
be strengthened by Me.

Take care to miss Me not.
Watch and listen.
My face appears.
My voice is being heard.
Know Me as your Master and Friend, Teacher and
Brother, Guide and Messenger of God.

May the Divine Light and Love and Power of the
One Most Holy God be now manifest within your
hearts and minds.
May this manifestation lead you to see yourselves
and each other as the Gods you are.

Message No. 100

March 19th 1980

My dear friends, I am happy to be with you at
this centenary, as you might call it.

My friends, I am near you indeed.
I see around you your aspiration and love, your
hope and desire for a better world.
Believe Me, My friends, all these will be
fulfilled.
That New World is now in the making, is formed
in thought and desire, and slowly descends.
Therefore, My brothers, know no fear.

I am among you in many ways.
I present Myself to the world in many facets.
I galvanize all forms to change.
I stimulate all souls to growth.
I am with you and in you.
I am the Heart of your life.
I seek to place before you the Laws which are God.
I aim to evoke from you the love of your heart.

I am the Prince of Peace.
I am the Sword Bearer.
I am in your hearts as Love.
I am your Friend and Guide.
I am the Lawgiver.
I know God's Purpose.
I teach His Plan.
I long to serve.
I greet the New Day.
I bring Joy.
I awaken the New Spirit in man.
I come prepared for My task.
I call you as helpers.
I take you by the hand to the Source.
I shall live among you.

My Teaching goes forth.
The New Day beckons.
The Real takes root.
The Time of God has come.
My Way beckons all men.
My Travail will not be in vain.
My Justice shall be done.
My Army shall triumph.

By pure Love man will achieve.
By great deeds man will conquer.
By mighty steps man will advance into the future.
By My help all shall be achieved.

My name is Oneness.
My Love abideth.
My Law creates.
My Teaching shall turn all men to God.

My Masters stand ready.
The Day is at hand.
The Prophecies of Old are being fulfilled.
The dark ones tremble.
The Law shall be upheld.
The Name of God is Love.
I am His Messenger.

May the Divine Light and Love and Power of the
One Most Holy God be now manifest within your
hearts and minds.
May this manifestation lead you quickly to see
yourselves as Units of God.